Yet Not I But Christ

by Samuel Hayes Sherwood

© Copyright 2018 Samuel Hayes Sherwood

ISBN 978-1-7323109-2-6

All rights reserved. No part of this publication may be reproduced, stored in a retrieval system, or transmitted in any form or by any means – electronic, mechanical, photocopy, recording, or any other – except for brief quotations in printed reviews, without the prior written permission of the author.

Published by

SHERWOOD
PRESS

yetnotibutchrist.com

Yet Not I
But
Christ

Samuel Hayes Sherwood

SHERWOOD
PRESS

TABLE OF CONTENTS

I.	In The Beginning, God ...
II.	What Just Happened?
III.	The Mystery Which is Christ in Us
IV.	Where Does God Dwell?
V.	Are You Perfect?
VI.	The Two Nature Myth
VII.	Then Why Do We Sin?
VIII.	What Is Sin?
IX.	The Self-Improvement Myth
X.	Dividing Asunder Between Soul and Spirit
XI.	The Meaning of Life
XII.	The Tree of Life
XIII.	What is Marriage All About?
XIV.	Buried with Him, Raised with Him
XV.	The Lord's Supper
XVI.	Water to Wine
XVII.	Passover — A Spiritual Allegory
XVIII.	Can You Fly?
XIX.	Do you hate Hypocrites?
XX.	The Fear of the Lord
XXI.	Is Gun Control the Answer?
XXII.	Faith or Works?
XXIII.	Faith or Positive Thinking?
XXIV.	Why Bother Praying?
XXV.	Count it all joy—Really?

XXVI.	Is There a Rest for the People of God?
XXVII.	To Deny or Not to Deny
XXVIII.	The Long Arm of the Law
XXIX.	Do You Have a Love Affair With the Law?
XXX.	Love IS God
XXXI.	Natural Disasters—An Act of God?
XXXII.	Who to Vote for—What Would Jesus Do?
XXXIII.	Have You Lost Your First Love?
XXXIV.	Atheism vs Theism
XXXV.	The Single Eye
XXXVI.	What Does Christ Look Like?
XXXVII.	What Does Satan Look Like?
XXXVIII.	In His Image
XXXIX.	If You Have Seen Me

I
IN THE BEGINNING, GOD ...

I HAVE many favorite verses, but I think the most ominous, the most profound, is Genesis 1:1:

In the beginning, God created the heavens and the earth.

It's not the act of creation I find so compelling but the clear implication that in the beginning, nothing existed but God. Nothing! And if nothing existed but God, then it has to be a fact that nothing that does exist, whether visible or invisible, exists outside of God. That means the earth, moon, rocks—you name it—and all forms of life whether perceived as good or evil exist only in God. Even the devil has no existence outside of God. God made him. Everything in its essence is a manifestation of the One Spirit, the One Person in the universe, whether positive or negative.

Since God is Spirit, He has no form or expression in His essence. Therefore He must express Himself through that which He creates. His first act of creation, as far as we know, is that of the heavens and the earth. This He does through His Word, which dwelt with Him before the world was (John 17:5). The Spirit (Father) spoke it into existence through His Word (Son) and made it happen through His Holy Spirit.

Now consider how ominous this is, what is being said. In the beginning, the only "thing" that existed was a Person. And that was God. Therefore, it can be clearly concluded that that is still true. Only One Person still exists in the universe ... God, and there is nothing that exists other than God.

Consider the Law of Conservation of Mass and Energy, amended by Einstein, but authored by none other than God. It states that mass and energy in a closed system must remain constant over time. You can convert one to the other but you cannot take away or add to. That simply means that all things, visible or invisible, good or evil, were created out of the only thing that existed in the beginning ... God. You cannot add to or takeaway from God. It is an immutable law of the universe.

If that is true, then all of us, believers and non-believers alike, find that we are nothing more than a manifestation, a derivative of and a unique expression of God. Acts 17:28 confirms this saying,

... for " 'In him we live and move and have our being'; ...

So what does it really mean? For one thing, the concept of being independent persons, separate and distinct from God, cannot be true. That is an illusion; it's a delusion promulgated by Satan himself who actually believes he can work independently and in opposition to God and replace Him. "I will set my throne on high," he said (Isa 14:13).

It means that we, who are in Christ, are one with God and one with each other. It means that those who oppose God are still in God, albeit in a negative form, blinded to the truth, separated only by their unbelief.

It means that we who believe can say as Paul did, "I am crucified with Christ: nevertheless I live; yet not I, but Christ liveth in me: ..." (Gal 2:20)

Think about it. *I live, yet not I, but Christ.* The lines are blurred. It sounds like double speak. Who is living here? Him or me? It's both. It's two yet one. We are in a union with Christ. It's the mystery which is Christ in us (Col 1:27). It's more than just He "in" us. He manifests Himself "as" us in the many individual human forms that we see. We are the Branch. He is the Vine. We are immutably joined in union to Him, one with Him, and therefore manifesting Him on earth.

II

WHAT JUST HAPPENED?

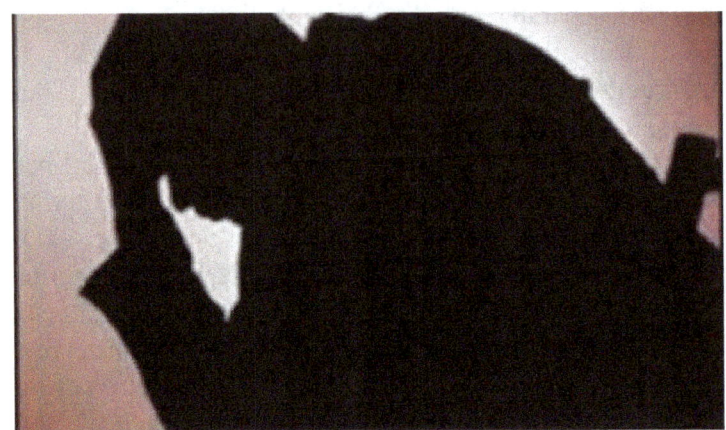

DID YOU ever have one of those *"What Just Happened"* moments? Where you pushed the wrong button, made the wrong decision, said the wrong thing and before you could take it back—BOOM?! You were past the point of no return! No way to back out! Well, there was a time in our history when the entire known world was rocked by one Jim Dandy of a *"What Just Happened"* moment. That was in the Garden of Eden. The Good News, though, was that there was a way back provided by our Creator.

Let's go back to the beginning in the Garden and see what happened. Things were pretty good back then, were they not? Adam and Eve were bebopping through the garden naked without a care in the world. Life was pretty easy. You could say they were childlike, not unlike the kingdom of heaven described by Jesus:

... but Jesus said, "Let the little children come to me and do not hinder them, for to such belongs the kingdom of heaven." (Matt 19:14)

And everything was Good:

And God saw everything that he had made, and behold, it was very good. (Gen 1:31)

Why was it good? Did evil not exist? Like children, they saw everything with the single eye, as good (Luke 11:34). They naturally flourished and bloomed, firmly rooted in God.

So what was the problem with all that good stuff? Well, they started to think about it. Instead of a *"...Take no thought for your life, what ye shall eat, or what ye shall drink; nor yet for your body, what ye shall put on ..." (Matt 6:25)* mentality they were deceived into thinking there was something even better. Along came Satan with enticements. They started to think ... to rationalize. They listened to someone other than God.

But the serpent said to the woman, "You will not surely die. For God knows that when you eat of it your eyes will be opened, and you will be like God, knowing good and evil." (Gen 3:4-5)

Then what happened? They bought it lock, stock, and barrel. After all, what was wrong with wanting to be like God?

And when the woman saw that the tree was good for food, and that it was pleasant to the eyes, and a tree to be desired to make one wise, she took of the fruit thereof, and did eat, and gave also unto her husband with her; and he did eat. (Gen 3:6)

So did they die? It looks like a yes and no answer. A simple way to look at it is as if we were removed from the life giving root and set in a vase.

We're still pretty though, right? For a while anyway, but let's not kid ourselves ... it's dead! Just temporarily on life support. And look at all we got for it. Now we know Good and Evil, but with a distorted and divided view that has resulted in about every kind of evil imaginable. We have this exaggerated sense of self-awareness and self-importance as evidenced by the sudden shame in their nakedness. The delusion of independent self had set in.

This metaphor shows what happened to us physically, to the body, but believe it or not, that's the last of our problems. Spiritually there was no grace period. When they ate of the apple, they died spiritually ... right then, right there. Instantaneously! Dead at the scene! Separated from god!

Man is designed to be nothing more than a receptacle, a container. He is referred to metaphorically as a vessel, jar of clay, and so on. He was meant to contain someone and that someone was God. God was meant to reside in us.

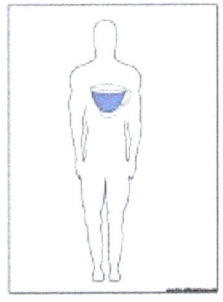

We were "Married" to, in Union with, GOD

Picture our spirit as a cup located in our heart. Prior to the fall, we were joined to and in union with God. He filled the cup.

When we rejected God, we didn't become independent persons. We just exchanged one owner for another and became joined to and in union

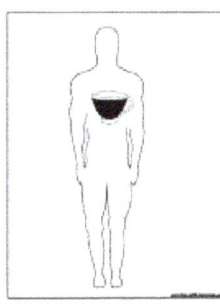

When we died, we became "Married" to, in Union with, ANOTHER

The "Container" does not change, just the contents

with the not-god who by nature is sin. He filled the empty cup and we then expressed that new nature.

So, now you know *What Just Happened*. Now we're stuck. The problem is we can't extricate ourselves from this new union. But there is one who can ... Jesus Christ. There is only one little thing we have to do. We have to die one more time. To make it easy, He did it for us. When Jesus died on the cross, we died also. We hung there with him in some mystical way that the human mind will never understand. All it takes is to believe in the one and only Son. And when you do, you are freed from your old husband and free to marry another (Rom 7:1-4) ... the One who we were meant to be married to. Then we can truthfully speak the meme, "Free at last, free at last, Thank God almighty we are free at last."

III

THE MYSTERY WHICH IS CHRIST IN US

I HAVE been teaching adult Bible Study for several years, mostly to senior adults. Without fail, regardless of the topic or the scripture, the lesson always circles back to the essence of what Christianity is all about—the mystery hidden for ages and generations but now revealed to his saints which is Christ in you (Col 1:26-27). It's a gravitational pull that keeps bringing us back to the same answer, over and over revealing the mystery of this profound truth of the gospel—the "Good News."

It's not that this mystery is new. It just seems that way. This week's lesson was titled *United with Christ*. The writer mentions how unfortunate it is that the doctrine of "union with Christ" doesn't get a lot of attention. I wonder if he knows just how right he is.

Jesus was clear how it works:

*"I am the true vine, and my Father is the vinedresser. ² Every branch in me that does not bear fruit he takes away, and every branch that does bear fruit he prunes, that it may bear more fruit. ³ Already you are clean because of the word that I have spoken to you. ⁴ Abide in me, and I in you. As the branch cannot bear fruit by itself, unless it abides in the vine, neither can you, unless you abide in me. ⁵ I am the vine; you are the branches. Whoever abides in me and I in him, he it is that bears much fruit, for **apart from me you can do nothing**.*"
(John 15:1-8)

Now any well-read Christian can quote these scriptures off the top of his/her head. The problem comes down to, when we utter these words, do we really "know" what they mean to us personally? Like so many overused words, phrases, and scriptures, at some point they become trite and lose their meaning. Scripture and answers are often parroted back without knowing their true meaning. "Born again" is an example of a term that has become trite. Everyone uses this term, but do they really know what born again means?

It is admirable to know the Bible and to be able to quote scriptures. The answers are right there. But that doesn't mean everyone sees them. Only God can give us eyes that see and ears that hear.

There is no shortage of material out there about how to live the Christian life. The problem is so much of it just scratches the surface. It's a mile wide and an inch deep, authored by a mental knowledge of the scriptures lacking the deep down knowledge that defies words.

So let's start with one fundamental truth. Christianity is not a way of life. It is Life! That may seem like a little nuance, a play on words, but it is critically important. We began with John 15 and that is what it is telling us. We can pull any another scripture and examine it closely and, if you have eyes to see, it will say the same thing.

Since the topic is "Union with Christ," let's pull some other scriptures that solidify what we are talking about. Paul says,

"I am crucified with Christ: nevertheless I live; yet not I, but Christ liveth in me: and the life which I now live in the flesh I live by the faith of the Son of God, who loved me, and gave himself for me (Gal 2:20)."

Another well used scripture. But does it quicken? I mean, does something deep down inside of you jump for joy when you read these words whether or not you completely understand? If not, don't worry. God reveals all in His due time.

Let's take another verse which puts it all in a nutshell, one of my favorites:

But he who is joined to the Lord becomes one spirit with him. (1Cor 6:17)

Another profound verse in the Bible. It says that if we are in union with Christ, if we are joined to him, we are ONE spirit with Him! Not two! ONE!

Like Christ was one with God, so now we are one with Christ. And if one, we already abide in him. We don't have to try to abide. Christ did it all. Jesus said,

> *" ... that they may all be one, just as you, Father, are in me, and I in you, that they also may be in us, so that the world may believe that you have sent me"* (John 17:21).

I know when we get into verses like this that things start to get very lofty and esoteric, but it is all right there staring us in the face. We just need to ask God to lift the veil that we might truly see all He has done for us and He has done it all. Once we understand this union relationship, everything becomes easy. It no longer takes any effort. We bear fruit as a natural result of our abiding in Christ. He does the works. All we have to do is believe.

IV

WHERE DOES GOD DWELL?

WHEN YOU think of a temple, what comes to mind? A building? An ornately adorned cathedral? A mosque, synagogue, or tabernacle? A solemn place of worship?

And what about their purpose? Why do we have all these temples in the first place? Does God have a greater presence inside a temple than a block down the road? Is the ground more holy? Are we closer to God when we enter? I know people who certainly feel that way. But feelings don't really have much to do with where God is or is not. In fact, He is everywhere in the same measure. There is no place He is not.

> *If I ascend up into heaven, thou art there: if I make my bed in hell, behold, thou art there.* (Ps 139:8 KJV)

Whether plain or grandiose monuments, their function is the same—a place for people to gather and worship their god or gods. They have no real spiritual significance with one exception: the Temple in Jerusalem. Why is this one different?

When Moses built the first tabernacle, or the place of dwelling, he was told by God exactly how to build it.

"The people must make a sacred Tent for me, so that I may live among them. ⁹ Make it and all its furnishings according to the plan that I will show you." (Ex25:8-9)

The first Temple was also built according to plans David received from God. So what is so different about this pattern as opposed to all the other temples?

As we discuss this, remember that symbolism, allegories, and metaphors are the way God communicates to us heavenly things in earthly terms. It is no different with the temple.

"The work they do as priests is really only a copy and a shadow of what is in heaven. It is the same as it was with Moses. When he was about to build the Sacred Tent, God told him, 'Be sure to make everything according to the pattern you were shown on the mountain.'" (Heb 8:5)

There are many things going on regarding this temple, but we are only going to look at one aspect. It had three parts: the courtyard, the Holy Place, and the Holy of Holies. The courtyard was available to all. The Holy Place was only accessed by the priests to make offerings and sacrifices. The Holy of Holies was entered only once a year on the Day of Atonement by the high priest to make offerings for himself and the unintentional sins of the people. A veil separated the Holy Place from the Holy of Holies.

The three parts correspond to the triune makeup of God—God the Father (Spirit), the Son (Word), and the Holy Spirit. Man likewise is triune—spirit, soul, and body. The temple is more than the dwelling place of God. It is the image of God. And of us made in His image!

God is Spirit and his dwelling place is the Holy of Holies. It contained the Ark of the Covenant in which were placed the Tablets of the Covenant (the Ten Commandments). These things symbolize the promises of God and His true nature which is Love.

That might seem contradictory since the law doesn't seem all that forgiving, but Love is the only way to fulfill the law. That is how Jesus did it. For us, the law is a problem because we cannot keep it. That is what the veil represents. That is what separates us from God.

Make no mistake; God wants to dwell in union with our spirits, not in some dank and dark room.

God, who made the world and everything in it, is Lord of heaven and earth and does not live in temples made by human hands. (Acts 17:24)

He has other ideas. Something had to be done to remove the barrier.

The solution is Jesus Christ. When He died on the cross, in some mysterious and actual way, we also died ... if we believe. When we died, we were freed from our old union and free to marry another—Christ. When that union occurs, the veil is split from top to bottom and the law now becomes what it was meant to be, pure Love. The reason we are no longer under the written law is because the true law now dwells in us. On the day you believe, this is fulfilled in you:

> *"For this is the covenant that I will make with the house of Israel after those days, declares the Lord: I will put my law within them, and I will write it on their hearts. And I will be their God, and they shall be my people."* (Jer 31:33)

That is why Paul has to remind us.

> *"Do you not know that you are God's temple and that God's Spirit dwells in you?"* (1Cor 3:16)

That is why there is no longer a temple in Jerusalem. It is no longer necessary. It was a shadow of things to come. Those things are here ... now ... you.

We no longer try to fulfill the law. We are the law. We let Christ fulfill it. It's easy, because we no longer live. He lives in us.

> *I am crucified with Christ: nevertheless I live; yet not I, but Christ liveth in me: and the life which I now live in the flesh I live by the faith of the Son of God, who loved me, and gave himself for me.* (Gal 2:20)

V

ARE YOU PERFECT?

"I'M NOT perfect." Ever hear anyone say that? And of course there is the classic—"No one is perfect. We all make mistakes." This comes out of almost everyone's mouth. I expect to hear such talk from non-Christians. After all, that is their main excuse to justify themselves and point out that they are, after all, as good as anyone else, including Christians.

But when Christians say it, I cringe. They often add, "I'm not perfect *but* I'm getting better every day," with the Lord's help, of course. Any time the word "but" is used, it pretty much negates anything before.

Prayer meetings are speckled with confessions of failure with the implication to try harder. "Forgive us Lord when we fail. Help us to do better." Undaunted by their continual failures, many believe they are making progress in their quest to improve.

This is the problem I have with only being imperfect—it leaves a lot of wiggle room. It's not much of a confession; it doesn't go far enough. What it implies is yes, I am imperfect, but I am not that bad and the door is open for me to get better and better—room to improve. Pride lurks on the other side of that statement.

Now, anyone who believes they are getting better every day is feeding themselves a lie. Let me give you a secular example. I spent years in management. The expectation is always to drive continuous improvement and have it validated by real metrics. I remember my first real management position. For the first five years I heard my staff tell me over and over, "We are getting better." We would have a bad month then a good one, a bad one then a good one. It was usually during the good months I heard this but the bad months didn't preclude anyone from believing. It was a repetitive cycle.

One day I decided to find out the truth. I gathered data as far back as I could, my five years plus ten years before me. I did an analysis to determine if there was any statistical change over time, either good or bad. Guess what I found? Well, we weren't getting any worse. That was good. But we also were not getting any better! It was flat lined. The reason this was true was because nothing had changed in the behavior of the process. All the "feelings" in the world could not contradict the facts.

If I could come up with metrics for continuous improvement in living the so-called Christian life, guess what I would find? The same thing! Why? Because there is no such thing as self-improvement! There is no scale. It's binary. It is an either/or situation.

"So what do you mean?" you ask. "Why can't we improve?"

Well, let me ask you a question—what is your metric? The only possible measure I can think of is compliance to the law or a set of rules, principles, or values, all of which are variable and argumentative. Immediately, I have to bring to your remembrance what brought us to Christ in the first place—the Law!

> *"For whoever keeps the whole law but fails in one point has become accountable for all of it."* (James 2:10)

And since it was never possible to keep the law ...

> *"... for all have sinned and fall short of the glory of God"* (Rom 3:23)

... either before or after knowing Christ as your Lord, then using that metric is going to get you an "F." It's binary. Either fulfill it all or forget it. No partial credit!

Another measure that might work is how we do relative to one another against a set of perceived values. That one is very popular amongst the elect and the non-elect. That might make us feel good until the backdrop of God's Law which is Love appears behind us and reminds us just who we are—a black silhouette against a blinding white canvas. This metric is borne out of pride, the most insidious spiritual cancer out there.

Let's cut to the chase. You may feel righteous at times, but what Isaiah said doesn't change with time:

> *"But we are all as an unclean thing, and all our righteousnesses are as filthy rags; ..."* (Isa 64:6 KJV)

The operative word here being *"our"* righteousness. Paul, one who could boast about coming closer than anyone to keeping the law, came to the same conclusion:

"[8]Indeed, I count everything as loss because of the surpassing worth of knowing Christ Jesus my Lord. For his sake I have suffered the loss of all things and count them as rubbish, in order that I may gain Christ [9] and be found in him, not having a righteousness of my own that comes from the law, but that which comes through faith in Christ, the righteousness from God that depends on faith— "(Phil 3:8-9)

"Ok," you say, "we have heard these things time and again. We got it. We're filthy. We feel bad. We're failures. Happy now?"

Well, no. What you need to understand is that if you are in Christ, it's totally not true! It is true is that the flesh is the same yesterday, today, and tomorrow. It doesn't change. If you try to be "good" then you are reverting back to being under the law. It didn't work then ... it doesn't work now, but it is an easy trap to fall into. The flesh may be dead but many keep trying to pump life back into it.

You see, you are not in the flesh. You are in the Spirit.

You, however, are not in the flesh but in the Spirit, if in fact the Spirit of God dwells in you. Anyone who does not have the Spirit of Christ does not belong to him. (Rom 8:9)

You are no longer filthy, depraved, or lawless. You are already perfect. How? Because your "filthy" righteousness has been replaced by Christ's. Your spirit and His Spirit are joined together and are now ONE Spirit. ONE! Not two!

> *"But he who is joined to the Lord becomes one spirit with him." (1Cor 6:17)*

Because of that fact, you ARE the righteousness of God. This goodness that is in you is beyond comprehension. It means you don't have to try to be good ... you already are. How can you try to be something you already are? We are just vessels, jars of clay that contain the mystery of this treasure.

> *"But we have this treasure in jars of clay, to show that the surpassing power belongs to God and not to us." (2Cor 4:7)*

But, just like many will question that they were all that filthy evil before Christ, many cannot buy the notion of being all this righteous either just because we believed in Christ. They tend to be very sin conscious which means they haven't yet freed themselves from the law despite the fact they can quote Romans backwards and forwards:

> *"For sin will have no dominion over you, since you are not under law but under grace." (Rom 6:14)*

The reason most cannot fully appreciate the extent of this gift is because they don't fully appreciate the depth from which they were redeemed. They return to the law like a dog returns to its vomit. That might be a little sickening to picture, but believe me that is much prettier than what it really is. Jesus said that we were clean. Maybe we have to wash our feet, but there is no more work to be done. Get over it.

At the end of the day, all we have is Christ. When we come to the conclusion that only Christ can live like

Christ, and that is taken care of by the fact that we no longer live, but Christ lives in us, then we will have put our own works away and arrived at true rest.

"I am crucified with Christ: nevertheless I live; yet not I, but Christ liveth in me: and the life which I now live in the flesh I live by the faith of the Son of God, who loved me, and gave himself for me." (Gal 2:20 KJV)

VI

THE TWO NATURE MYTH

JESUS SAID, "I have yet many things to say unto you, but ye cannot bear them now." (John 16:12)

This verse has always intrigued me because it is telling us that there must be something far more to our faith than we can see or are able to accept. That forces me to seek out things that deepen faith, that go beyond the mainstream teaching. I just know there is more and I want it!

Here is one truth that most Christians have difficulty accepting: The notion of having two natures is a myth!

Now I can see eyebrows raised in skepticism. Let's face it, most people struggle with the angel and devil caricatures standing on our shoulders. The angel is whispering in one ear to do good, resist temptation, while the devil yells in the other, "What for? Wutt'l it hurt?"

Let's put that image aside and deal with scripture and the facts. That is all we have to rely on. Here is what James says:

> *"Does a fountain send out from the same opening both fresh and bitter water? Can a fig tree, my brethren, produce olives, or a vine produce figs? Nor can salt water produce fresh."* (James 3:11-12)

Regardless of how you "feel," James says it is impossible for two natures to coexist in us. It's one or the other. An orange tree cannot produce apples and vice versa. We can only be one thing. So, what nature do we have? Peter says:

> *"Whereby are given unto us exceeding great and precious promises: that by these ye might be partakers of the divine nature,..."* (2 Pet 1:4)

There you have it—we are partakers of the "divine" nature. You would think problem solved, but the obvious question everyone is going to ask is if that is true, why do we still struggle with sin? If this one nature is so *Good*, why do we get stuck in Romans crying woes like this?

> *"O wretched man that I am! Who shall deliver me from the body of this death?"* (Rom 7:24)

Remember, Jesus was God, but he was also a man. He was tempted just like us. Yet he was without sin.

> *"... but One who has been tempted in all things as we are, yet without sin."* (Heb 4:15)

So how did He do it? Many try the WWJD (what would Jesus do?) mantra to avoid sin. But that is looking at it through the wrong end of the telescope. If you want to know how Jesus handled temptation, you have to look at WDJD (what did Jesus do). He gave us plenty of clues.

"No one sews a patch of unshrunk cloth on an old garment; otherwise the patch pulls away from it, the new from the old, and a worse tear results. No one puts new wine into old wineskins; otherwise the wine will burst the skins, and the wine is lost and the skins as well; but one puts new wine into fresh wineskins." (Mark 2:21-22)

The meaning is simple. It means that self-improvement is another myth! Trying to guess what Jesus would have done in a given situation is a formula for failure. Before our redemption we had no power to fulfill the law, to be good, and here is the revelation—you still don't! You haven't changed. The only thing that has changed is who indwells your spirit. You have no nature of your own. You take on the nature of who owns you.

That fact doesn't stop us as babes in Christ from constantly looking to improve ourselves, to impress others, to be better and stepping out into false righteousness. But what is the result? You know what the result is. We all do because all of us have tried over and over seemingly ad infinitum and failed. We end up like the Israelites in their endless cycle of sin and repentance!

So what is the answer? Well, it sounds like a contradiction, but this is how you emulate Christ—by NOT TRYING! This is how Jesus did it. He had no more power over sin than you do.

"So Jesus said to them, 'Truly, truly, I say to you, the Son can do nothing of his own accord, but only what he sees the Father doing. For whatever the Father does, that the Son does likewise.'" (John 5:19)

You see, Jesus rested in the fact that He was ONE with the Father.

"I and the Father are one."
(John 17:22)

In fact, He identified so much with the Father that He could say,

"He that hath seen me hath seen the Father."
(John 14:9)

That means that when He acted, it was God acting. When He spoke, it was God speaking.

Until you stop "trying" to be what you already are, until you realize that you and Christ are ONE and that the only righteousness you have is Him, you will always "feel" like you have two natures and be tricked into responding to temptation.

Until the meaning of this becomes completely clear,
...

"I am the vine, you are the branches; he who abides in Me and I in him, he bears much fruit, for apart from Me you can do nothing." *(John 15:5)*

... you will continue to struggle and be tricked into believing Romans 7:24, begging for a deliverance you already have. And we know who the trickster is and he is not some cute cartoon sitting on our shoulder. He is real and goes around seeking whom he may devour.

Believe this instead:

"But he who is joined to the Lord becomes one spirit with him." (1Cor 6:17)

Just as Jesus was ONE with the Father, so are we ONE with Christ! We are totally NEW! You can't be patched up. You can't put new wine into old wineskins. It has to be put into a new wineskin. Leave that phony notion of fixing yourself up behind. You are a new creation!

Abide in Him. Believe that He is able. Then you can say, "I can do nothing of my own accord, but only what I see Christ doing."

That is the only way it works!

VII

THEN WHY DO WE SIN?

IN THE previous article, *The Two Nature Myth*, I said that man has no nature of his own. He is simply a container and takes on the nature of whomever it is that indwells him. There are only two choices—God or the not-god. If we contain Christ, then we take on the nature of Christ. If this is so, the question we struggle with, admittedly myself also, is why do we still sin? As always, the only thing we can do is rely on scripture. We can start with what we know—we are:

> *"... predestined to become conformed to the image of His Son, ..."* (Rom 8:29)

We love verses like this, but the truth is, most of the time, we sure don't *feel* like we are conformed to anything remotely holy. Paul says forget feelings and ...

"... reckon ye also yourselves to be dead indeed unto sin, but alive unto God through Jesus Christ our Lord." (Rom 6:11)

Count it to be so. Whether you feel it or not. That is easy to say but we know it takes a lot of faith to dismiss all the appearances and feelings that seem to confirm the opposite. Like Abraham, we have to call into existence those things that are not as though they were (Rom 4:17). Just say (and believe) it's so. Jesus said,

"Do not judge according to appearance, but judge the righteous judgment." (John 17:24)

Not so easy to do, is it? To believe that we are conformed to the image of Christ regardless of appearances with all that evidence to the contrary. Usually we just feel condemned.

So why do we feel this way? There a few reasons. Mostly it is the misunderstanding that most of us have of the difference between soul and spirit (see the article *Dividing Asunder Between Soul and Spirit*). We need to know that though we are now in Christ, not much else has changed. We live in a cursed world:

"For we know that the whole creation groaneth and travaileth in pain together until now. And not only they, but ourselves also, which have the firstfruits of the Spirit, even we ourselves groan within ourselves, waiting for the adoption, to wit, the redemption of our body." (Rom 8:22-23)

Our spirits are redeemed, but our soul and body are still mired here on earth. And though we may be dead to sin, sin is most certainly not dead to us. Satan is still roaming around seeking whom he may devour and has plenty of tricks up his sleeve. He may not be working from the inside anymore, but he is equally talented working from the outside. Let's take a look at what I am talking about:

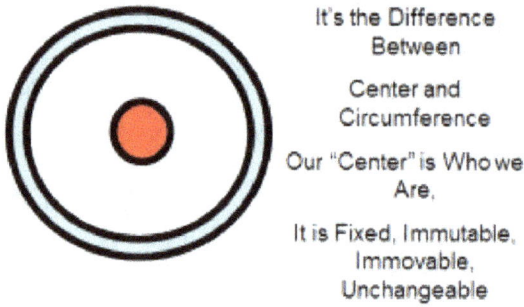

In the model above, the center is our spirit. It's fixed, immutable, unchangeable. That is where our spirit is joined to Christ and the two are one (1 Cor 6:17). The circumference is our body and soul, the part of us exposed to this fallen world.

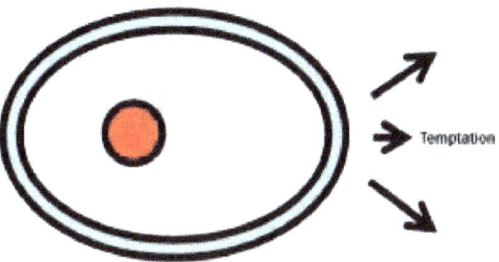

Temptation is NOT Sin

Satan, who knows us better than we do, works on the appetites of the body through temptation. He pulls on those appetites. Tempts us with them. But temptation is not sin. It's natural. Jesus was tempted in all ways as we yet without sin.

It is important to know there are no appetites of the body that are inherently evil. God put them all there to be *rightly* used. He didn't make a mistake. We are well engineered. But Satan knows how to pull them out of shape, what buttons to push, and tries to stretch them with the hope that we are lured and enticed enough to misuse them and give birth to sin. (James 1:15)

If we fall for that, we sin. Nevertheless, that doesn't make us any less joined to Christ. The only way out is to recognize who we are in Christ and realize it is only Him who is able.

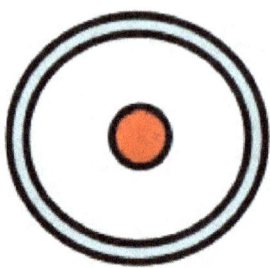

Once we recognize, or remember, who we are and that we don't have to respond, it will snap back just like a rubber band. And if we should sin, we recognize it as such, confess it and let it go. Satan loves it when we beat up on ourselves and gladly helps you out with the flogging because that quenches the Spirit more than anything. On the other hand, God has forgotten. You're the only one left who remembers. So, if you revert back to:

"Wretched man that I am! Who will deliver me from this body of death?" (Rom 7:24)

Then remember as many times as you need to that the answer is ...

"Thanks be to God through Jesus Christ our Lord!"
(Rom 7:25)

Count this to be so and see what happens!

VIII

WHAT IS SIN?

WHAT IS sin? Someone asked me that the other day. As I thought about it, I realized that it is really not a silly question. Many people grapple with it and opinions vary considerably. I spent much of my career working in Kentucky and West Virginia, an area you might call the gateway to the famous Bible Belt. The workers there belonged to quite a cadre of different fundamentalist churches. I remember we had a manager transferred from New Jersey and they were all eager to share their faith. After ignoring them for some time, he finally said, "Look. I can line all of you up against that wall and none of you will agree on anything." That was perceptive. He was right.

So what is sin? Drink'n, swear'n, and smok'n are staples on the Baptists' list. The Catholics have a list of venial and mortal sins too numerous to mention. Of course we all know the famous seven deadly sins—lust, gluttony, greed, sloth, wrath, envy, and pride. And let's not forget Paul's litany—sexual immorality, impurity, sensuality, idolatry, sorcery, enmity, strife, jealousy, fits of anger, rivalries, dissensions, divisions, envy, drunkenness, orgies, homosexuality, thievery, greed, adultery and the list goes on.

Wow! That's a wide net. Did we miss anyone ... uh ... I mean anything? It is amazing the pedantic interest in these behaviors that in themselves are nothing more than symptomatic of a deeper disorder that seems to evade our understanding. Focusing on *sins* is once again looking at it through the wrong end of the telescope. We have to get out of the weeds and understand where sins have their source. To do that, we need to start with the fifty thousand foot level definition of sin. John gives us a simple definition.

Sin is Lawlessness (1 John 3:4)

Now, I doubt anyone is going to say, "Ahhh, I see. I get it." No, probably not. They are going to say you're quoting some esoteric scripture that sounds lofty and all, but what does it mean to me? Well, you have to understand what the law is really all about. You remember that God gave the original law to Moses, then added several more rules and regulations, and then man in his eternal desire to be like God added a bunch more. We became a nation of laws. We operate under the so-called Rule of Law.

So now we are civilized people. We are good people. Why do we think that? Because we, more or less, observe the law or at least most try. We feel pretty good about it. There is just one problem with all these laws—*Laws are for the lawless!* They wouldn't exist if man's nature was always to do the right thing, to live for others and not for self which is the nature of God. No, they are there because man's innate nature is to do the opposite. Their existence is an indictment against mankind! That may sound quite simplistic but this is your first clue to the problem!

You see, the external law does not address the source. It doesn't cure the disease. It was never meant to. The law, as we know it, is a dumbed down version for human consumption to show us something spiritual and something about ourselves. It's an earthly replica of something in heaven.

Before we get into the weeds again, let's get back up to the fifty thousand foot level to understand what the Law really is. It was given to man for two reasons. One was to reveal the true nature of God which is Love (1John 4:8). God is Love and God is the Law. We know that the only thing that fulfills the Law is Love (Rom 13:10). The Law and Love are two sides of the same coin.

The second reason it was given was not to make us better people. It was to reveal our true nature; to reveal the truth about ourselves that we do not have the Law in our hearts and therefore do not have love in our hearts. It was given so that we would recognize our fallen condition and realize our total helplessness and our need for God to save us. Not to save us from *sins*, but to save us from *Sin* which dwells in our hearts because of the original fall in the garden.

So back to the question. All this discussion about sin and what constitutes a sin is much ado about nothing. Now you can sit and debate and parse what is and what isn't sin but I am going to make this very simple—*everything is sin.* Even all your "good" works because unless the Word of God dwells in you, everything you do is for self. We are driven by the *self-for-self* sin nature we were born with. No exceptions. You can pretend it is not so, but there is no escape. It is who we are when we enter this world. Jesus didn't mince words.

You are of your father the devil, and your will is to do your father's desires. He was a murderer from the beginning, and does not stand in the truth, because there is no truth in him. When he lies, he speaks out of his own character, for he is a liar and the father of lies. (John 8:44)

Many will scoff at this. Others will gloss over this to clumsily justify themselves saying, "We were born this way. We had no choice, so how could what we do be a sin?" That's a good question. It has been answered.

^{19}You will say to me then, "Why does he still find fault? For who can resist his will?" ^{20} But who are you, O man, to answer back to God? Will what is molded say to its molder, "Why have you made me like this?"
(Rom 9:19-20)

The fact is we are all the same—born in Sin. I am no different than you and you are no different than I. None of us had a choice. There are no exceptions.

Behold, I was brought forth in iniquity, and in sin did my mother conceive me. (Ps 51:5)

Now I am going to really make it simple. There is really only *ONE* sin! **The only sin is unbelief**—not believing in the one whom he has sent—Jesus Christ.

... and you do not have his word abiding in you, for you do not believe the one whom he has sent. (John 5:38)

The truth is that even though we had no choice in the condition in which we were born, afterwards we do have a choice. We can remain where we are and make excuses or we can choose the free gift of grace offered to us in Jesus Christ and then our Sin nature is replaced by God's nature which is love.

*¹⁵ The Holy Spirit also testifies to us about this. First he says: ¹⁶"This is the covenant I will make with them
after that time, says the Lord.
I will put my laws in their hearts,
and I will write them on their minds." (Heb 10:15-16)*

When we believe in Christ and receive him as Lord, He comes and dwells in our hearts. The law becomes an integral part of us and we now exhibit God's nature which is love—self for others. This is what Paul referred to *the mystery which is Christ in us (Col 1:27)*. We no longer need an external set of laws. We *are* the law. We *are* love because we are joined to God through Jesus Christ and become ONE with Him (1 Cor 6:17).

Now does that mean that Christians don't sin? No. It just means that it is no longer our nature to sin. Most do not fully understand this principle and those that do can still forget who they are in Christ and step out on their own only to be lured into submitting themselves back under the external law which ends in failure. That is the only way we can sin—Unbelief!

IX

THE SELF-IMPROVEMENT MYTH

A PRESIDENTIAL candidate from a prominent political family recently stated religion "ought to be about making us better as people." Really?

I have a pretty good idea that that view is shared by a large proportion of Christians. This is not surprising since the trend today, under the smokescreen of religious tolerance and acceptance, is to homogenize all religion. They are all the same; the same god with different names and faces. However, if you share that view, then you have pooled Christianity with all the false world religions and made it part of the ten billion dollar self-improvement industry which, well ... really cheapens it.

False, you say? Well that is very narrow-minded and bigoted, even hateful. What makes you Christians better? Well, actually nothing. That is the whole point.

First of all, if you signed up for Christianity, then you should be aware of the one major difference between it and every single one of the world religions. It is true that all others purpose to make people better, or appear better, through personal effort and/or compliance to a set of codes. Christianity doesn't do that. You can try to modify and control behavior with some modicum of results, but man, in his human essence, has not the ability to improve himself. That means that there are no high and mighty Christians. Actually, it's the opposite. It's the lowly, the poor in spirit who come.

Christianity is based on the truth that man cannot save himself. It is totally outside of our grasp to improve ourselves. No effort, no achievement, no pedigree, no amount of charity or good works can change who we are or make us presentable to God. Sure, you have that degree from Harvard hanging on your office wall. You should be proud. But other than the fact you may have a good education, you are still you. That doesn't make you a better person, just more educated. Sorry.

So, let's cut to the chase. I had a manager once that was caught using his company computer to view porn. Guess he didn't know IT was policing the systems. They wanted to fire him. I remember him saying remorsefully, "I thought I was a good Christian person." Well, bless his heart, there is no such thing as "good Christian people."

What he didn't know is that man is neither good nor bad. He has no "nature" of his own. He doesn't have the capacity for either. Jesus said, "Why do you call me good? There is none good but God (Matt 19:17)." All He was saying was what you call good is simply the Father dwelling in Him. His human form was merely the earthly container for Him.

Man is no different. You see, like the Christ, our human forms are earthly containers, designed for someone to indwell. The choices are either the spirit of Satan or the Spirit of God. We all enter this world containing the former. There is the dilemma. There is no way to improve on Satan. He has no intention of improving himself. Now you can slap on some makeup, get educated, read all the self-improvement books, become more sophisticated, take some wine tasting classes, and even learn a new personality, but at the end of the day, you can't shake off that which is inextricably joined in union with your spirit. That is who you are. You are simply putting a gold ring in a pig's snout.

So what can you do? There is only one way out to change this bad arrangement. To change who you are you must replace the one who indwells you, the one who commandeered your life in the garden. Christ provided the only way for us.

What do we have to do? Simple. Just believe in Him. We don't change. We are still human containers. But the one who indwells us, the one our spirit is in union with, is replaced and we automatically take on that new nature. No effort. No striving. No adhering to do's and don'ts. No more having to hide who you are. No more pretending. We don't try to be good. Christ is that for us. That is His job. The liberated life begins.

X

DIVIDING ASUNDER BETWEEN SOUL AND SPIRIT

PROBABLY ONE of the things that mixes Christians up more than anything else is the confusion about who they really are, differentiating between soul and spirit. Paul says, *"For the word of God is living and active, sharper than any two-edged sword, piercing to the division of soul and of spirit, of joints and of marrow, and discerning the thoughts and intentions of the heart (Heb 4:12)."*

It is important to know the difference because if we confuse the two, we will ride a rollercoaster of highs and lows and wonder what is wrong with us when there isn't anything wrong. And it's not that simple to tell them apart. It takes the word of God to divide them.

So, just who exactly are we? To answer that question, we need to start with who God is. We know that he is tripartite—the trinity—the three Gods in one. I know that is beyond our reach of understanding and there are many explanations, most of which don't really quicken. But there is one image, perhaps simplistic, that can give us a better understanding.

First of all, God the Father is Spirit, and He seeks those to worship him in spirit and truth (John 4:24). This is the "WHO" of God, His essence. The problem with just the one part is spirit has no form or expression.

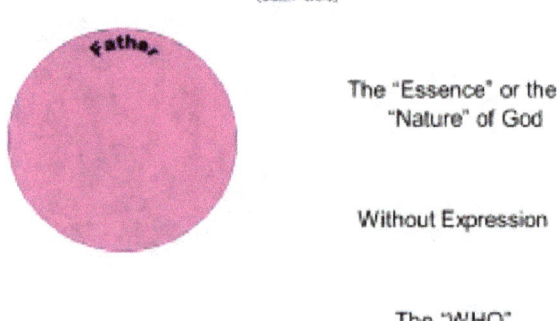

God must express himself. He manifests Himself through His Word. The reason Jesus was called the Word of God is because He is the exact representation, the expression of His Spirit Being (Heb 1:3). Think about it. How do we express ourselves? Through our words. Thought, then word. Spirit, then Son. You might think of Him as the "WHAT" of God.

GOD (SPIRIT) MUST MANIFEST HIMSELF (COL 1:15)

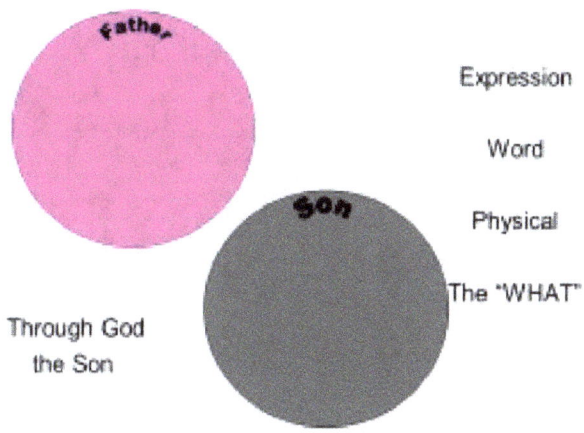

To complete the manifestation of Himself, He must also act. That is through the Holy Spirit. He is the "HOW" of God. *And the Spirit of God was hovering over the surface of the waters (Gen 1:2).*

GOD MUST ACT

Another way of looking at the composition of God is:

THE COMPOSITION OF GOD

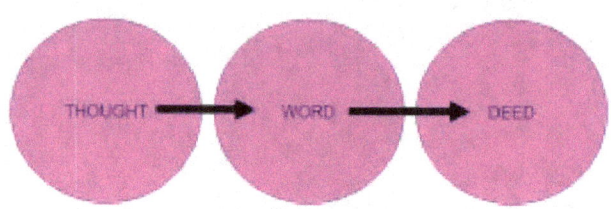

Put it all together and this is what you end up with: Thought—Word—Deed. Think it, say it, do it.

Now, let's look at man. He is made in God's image (Gen 1:27). So how does that work? To start with, we are also tripartite—spirit, soul, body. The spirit is also who we are, our essence, where it all starts. The soul is where we express our thoughts, our spirit, our word. It is the interface between the spirit and the world. The body is ... well you know. That is how we get it done. Look familiar?

And if we look at the composition of man another way, how about this? Looking a lot the same, huh?

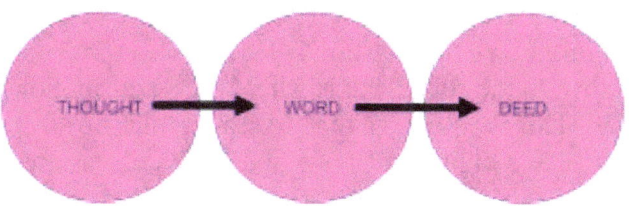

How about that? Thought—Word—Deed. We think it, we say it, we do it. When God said he created man in His own image, he was serious.

Now that we can visualize the parts, let's get to the problem between soul and spirit. If we mistake one for the other, we have trouble.

First, the human spirit is the real *SELF*. That is who we are. Soul and body are merely the clothing for the spirit, the expression of the spirit. It is just like the Son (Word) and the Holy Spirit are the expression of God the Spirit. The human spirit is where the heart, mind, and will reside. The heart is a euphemism for the center of our being. It is the container for God's Spirit and is therefore Love, if in fact we are in Christ. The mind is where we know things, and by that I mean all the mysteries of Christ and the universe. 1 Cor 2:16 says, "*We have the mind of Ch*rist." That is how we know. Before you go out bragging about how you know everything or start hunting down Alex Trebek, you better consider that the dissemination of that knowledge is limited by the measure of God's grace and revelation.

Now, the will is where we make our choices. The most important one is for Christ. And if we choose Christ, our will is to do God's will. If not Christ, it is the will of the not-god. Our spirit, our self, takes on the nature and will of the one it contains. That is the only nature we have. We have no nature of our own. That is a delusion.

Now, to the soul. That is where we have emotions and reason. This is where we tend to react to the world around us. We have highs and lows. We have depressions. It is variable. Our spirit is not variable. Like God is the same today, yesterday, and forever, so is our spirit.

Herein lays the problem. Our soul emotions are subject to inputs from the still small voice of our spirit and the loud clamor of our external environment. The question is which one are you going to believe? If we take all these changing feelings as reality, then we get whipped around like the wind, questioning ourselves, our motives, our heart, and eventually falling into the trap of self-condemnation. Many of our soul feelings are illusory.

For example, you may think you cannot love this person or that. In fact, you might feel like you hate him or her. Of course that can't be true. We just said if you are in Christ that your spirit center is love because God resides there. The truth is love is not a feeling. Love is actually a person, and that person is God, and God dwells in you in Christ. You cannot "not" love. It's not a matter of whether or not you "feel" you can love another; Christ does it through you, as you.

How about that? We keep circling back to the same verse that explains the way.

"I am crucified with Christ: nevertheless I live; yet not I, but Christ liveth in me: ..." (Gal 2:20)

To learn more about the difference between Soul and Spirit, I recommend *God Unlimited* by Norman Grubb.

XI

THE MEANING OF LIFE

MAN NEVER tires of asking the same old questions. What is life all about? Who is God? Does He exist at all? If He does exist, just where is He? Why doesn't He show Himself?

The questions are actually very good. God has instilled that curiosity in us so that we would seek the answer, seek Him. According to Jesus, the truth is available.

> *So Jesus said to the Jews who had believed him, "If you abide in my word, you are truly my disciples, and you will know the truth, and the truth will set you free."*
> *(John 31:31-32)*

However, that's apparently easier said than done because mankind and philosophers are still searching for the seemingly elusive answer though hidden in plain sight. The best they can come up with is *I think, therefore I am*.

Jesus talked about them also.

"always learning and never able to arrive at a knowledge of the truth." (2Tim 3:7)

Why is it so hard? Probably more than not most identify with the frustration of Pontius Pilot who asked the age old question, "What is truth?"

So, what is the truth? How do we find out who and where God is? Well, God is infinite so I certainly cannot fathom the depths of God. But we can answer the question in the limited context of what his purpose is for us—mankind. That means, of course, we need to know the mystifying purpose of life. Why were we created and why are we here? Until we know who we are, we are limited in truly knowing God.

What are we missing? I hate clichés, but I have to employ one here because sometimes *"we can't see the forest for the trees."*

Let me give an example.

Philip said to him, "Lord, show us the Father, and it is enough for us." Jesus said to him, "Have I been with you so long, and you still do not know me, Philip? Whoever has seen me has seen the Father. How can you say, 'Show us the Father.'?" (John 14:8-9)

Wow! How did they miss that? I guess they didn't see the forest for the trees, huh? There they were walking for three years with the embodiment and perfect expression of who God is and they didn't recognize Him. So what did they see? What were they looking for? They saw the *man* Jesus but they did not see the Christ. Hmmmm ... interesting.

That might make us wonder what else we are missing. It's not very far according to Paul.

"The word is near you, in your mouth and in your heart"
(Rom 10:8)

He says the word, the truth, is right there in you. If it's that near, we should be able to see it, but somehow we keep missing it. What is the problem? What is it we see? We walk around looking for God and all the while He is staring us right in the face waving His hands saying, "Wake up. See Me!"

Let's dig a little further and see what we may be missing. Many think that the sole purpose of man was simply for God to have a companion. While that certainly has an element of truth, it is much more than that, much deeper. God created man to dwell in, to join Himself to, to express Himself through. We are simply vessels created to contain the eternal God.

I'm not sure when Jesus said, "If you have seen me you have seen the Father," why he had to spell it out, but he did. They didn't get it. So in the same way, it appears we need to spell out the rest of the truth or we won't get it either. The further truth simply put means if you abide in Christ then you can say in like fashion, "If you have seen me, you have seen Christ." And if you have seen Christ, then you have seen the Father.

Now that is a mighty bold statement and not all are ready to accept it. You might say, "That is not in Scripture." Well, I beg your pardon. It may not be in those specific words, but verse after verse is screaming it out. Keep in mind that before Jesus spelled out who He was it was right there glaring in their faces.

Let's get out of the weeds and see the obvious. God created man so that He could dwell on earth in His creation and enjoy His creation through us. Jesus said,

"In my Father's house are many mansions: if it were not so, I would have told you. I go to prepare a place for you." (John 14:2)

Now if you think there is a three story brick colonial with columns waiting for you, think again. He is saying that God has created dwelling places for Himself. Those dwelling places are people, and those people are those that believe. You are those mansions. Paul spells it out.

"Do you not know that you are God's temple and that God's Spirit dwells in you?" (1Cor 3:16)

Do you not also know that when God comes to dwell in you that you become ONE with God?

"But he who is joined to the Lord becomes one spirit with him." (1Cor 6:17)

One spirit! Not two! One! And if one, then when I see you, I see Christ, the one you are in union with. That is why I can say in the current age that I live, yet not I, but Christ, just like Paul.

"I am crucified with Christ: nevertheless I live; yet not I, but Christ liveth in me" (Gal 2:20)

And then John spells it out again at the end of the age.

And I heard a loud voice from the throne saying, "Behold, the dwelling place of God is with man. He will dwell with them, and they will be his people, and God himself will be with them as their God." (Rev 21:3)

God does not mince words. The dwelling place of God is with man, but more specifically *IN* man. Man is the dwelling place of God. I doubt we will see an old man with a long white beard sitting on a throne in heaven. He will be there in all of us. The chaff will be gone and He will be expressing Himself through His ultimate creation—man. That was His purpose all along.

And that in a nutshell is the mystery which is Christ in you (Col 1:27).

XII

THE TREE OF LIFE

    A JEWISH friend of mine who purported to understand Christianity told me an interesting story. It was about the first sermon he remembered hearing from his Rabbi. First of all, let me say that his understanding is probably not much different than many Christians, so let's be careful about judging. Now, I have taken some literary license to make it read better. Here goes:

    "Once upon a time, there were two men who died," the Rabbi started. "When they awoke, they were sitting in front of the entrance gates to heaven. But they were not free. They were bound with cords opposite to one another, face to face. In between them lay two apples from the Tree of Life. Each could reach the apples with their hands, but their wrists were restrained in such a way that prevented them from bringing the fruit to their own mouths. The cords did not restrict them, however, from reaching their apple to the mouth of the other man. They looked at each other quizzically. What is this all about, they wondered?

"An angel appeared and spoke to the two men. 'You cannot enter the Kingdom of Heaven,' he said, 'unless you eat of the Tree of Life. I must now leave. If you are still here when I come back, it will be because you have not eaten of the Tree of Life and you will be cast into Hell. If you are not here when I come back, it will be because you have partaken of the Holy Fruit and been welcomed into heaven as one of God's faithful servants.' The angel disappeared before them.

"The two men stared at one another panicked. What would they do? They could not feed themselves. Each could see suspicion in the other's eyes as well as a reflection of their own distrust.

"When the angel came back, the two men were gone. They had eaten of the Tree of Life and entered the Kingdom of Heaven."

"How did they do it?" the Rabbi asked rhetorically. "They could not help themselves."

He waited a minute. There was silence.

"The answer is," explained the Rabbi, "that though they could not feed themselves, each could feed the other. In that moment, they had to put their faith in one another and put the Holy Fruit up to the other's mouth so the other could eat and enter heaven with no promise he would reciprocate."

"The moral of the story," the Rabbi said wrapping up his message, "is to do unto others as you would have done unto yourselves. This is what it is all about—doing good to others."

Now that story sounds very nice and noble. Many Christians would agree. That is what it is all about. After all, it is consistent with what Jesus said.

> *"And as you wish that others would do to you, do so to them."* (Luke 6:31)

But what if I were to tell you that it still falls short? It misses the mark. It's not enough. You might raise your eyebrows in bewilderment.

Let's examine this more closely. Paul said,

> *"For the whole law is fulfilled in one word: "You shall love your neighbor as yourself."* (Gal 5:14)

The operative word is *Love*! The question here is did these two men do it out of love, or did they do it with the idea of getting something back in return. If it was quid pro quo, it had no real merit according to Jesus.

> *"For if you love those who love you, what reward do you have?"* (Matt 5:46)

Let me explain what true love is by retelling the story with a little twist.

Let's say that one of the men in the story had his wrists bound behind his back. He could neither feed himself nor feed the other man. He was totally helpless. The other man was bound like the story above. He would be able to feed the other but not himself. That man was Jesus. He could save the man across from him, but there was no way that he would be able to partake. What would do you think the outcome would be now? Do you think there would have been one person, two persons, or none when the angel returned?

A trick question, you might ask? No. I think you know answer.

When the angel returned, he would have found one man remaining. That man is Jesus Christ. He is the only one that would die for another with no thought of anything in return. You see, the only way anyone will get to heaven is for God to provide a way, which he did through His Son, Jesus Christ. No one on earth has the power to get to heaven on their own by their own good works. We are totally helpless like the man in the revised story.

The only way we can get to heaven is to have Christ feed us from the Tree of Life which he did at the cost of his own life. Now that is what you call "True Self-Giving Love."

XIII

WHAT IS MARRIAGE ALL ABOUT?

I'M NO social activist. Jesus Christ was no social activist. He came, offered Himself as the Truth, spoke the truth and left it at that. He knew that truth needed no champion.

His stance on marriage was no different. There was no ambiguity in it. He loved to say, "It is written …" To Him, scripture revealed the immutable laws of God.

> [4] *He answered, "Have you not read that he who created them from the beginning made them male and female,* [5] *and said, 'Therefore a man shall leave his father and his mother and hold fast to his wife, and the two shall become one flesh'?* [6] *So they are no longer two but one*

flesh. What therefore God has joined together, let not man separate." (Matt 19:4-6)

That does not deter man from coming up with new and revised ideas of marriage to conform to the latest demands of today's society. Even the Supreme Court weighs in on the matter. But whenever the Supreme Court renders a 5-4 decision, when the greatest legal minds are split down the middle, it's clear it has nothing to with the law. The law may need clarification, but it isn't that gray. It just leans toward the latest thinking of a society as changeable as a suit of clothes. In fact, those black robes might as well be exchanged for the emperor's new clothes.

A quick google search on the origin of marriage babbles on how it evolved from animalistic polygamist sharing to its use in building alliances to social necessity and so on. Love ranked last, ignoring all of the day's band wagon pontificators on love and marriage. Being a simple minded person, I'll just go back to the true origin as documented in the Bible to which Jesus reminded the people of His day.

So what is marriage really all about? The true meaning goes far beyond the physical love and marriage and union of a man and a woman. It is actually symbolic of one of the greatest spiritual mysteries of all time.

To explain, I am going to take an excerpt from *The Lost Coin*, a Christian novel that I wrote in 2015. Sam, the protagonist, is searching for the true meaning of Christ in us. The setting is right after Sam has asked Mo to marry him. Mo, a knower of truth, engages him with a group of knowers who explain what marriage is really all about. Let's pick it up there with Mo asking Harry to explain:

"I think, Harry, if the group doesn't mind," she said looking around, *"that our engagement might be a great segue to talk about what marriage is really all about, what it means spiritually. You know, our union with Christ and why God said 'the two shall become one flesh.'"*

Sam nodded. *"I'd really like to know more about that."*

"Excellent topic," Harry began. *"Biblical marriage is another earthly picture of our union, our spiritual marriage to Christ."*

"Sorry, Harry, to be so dumb, but what do you mean our spiritual marriage to Christ?" Sam asked.

"There are no dumb questions, Sam," Harry said. *"Our earthly marriage is how God reveals something much greater, a heavenly truth—a spiritual marriage. Two becoming one flesh is a picture of two spirits becoming one spirit. Most don't realize but we have always been in a spiritual union. In the beginning, we, through Adam and Eve, were married to God. We were one with Him. When they ate of the apple, they rejected God and were tricked into a marriage union with Satan.*

"That is the miserable dilemma that all mankind has to start with. I say miserable, but the world at large has no idea that they are in this marriage or that it is all that bad. They buy into Satan's delusion of independence and that they can be good people on their own. Others realize that is impossible and earnestly crave a solution. But it's not so simple. We can't do it ourselves. Someone else has to do it for us. God provides that way.

"According to God's immutable Law, neither the earthly nor the spiritual union can be undone as long as we live. There is only one way out. Paul explains how in Romans 7— how through the Law we can be freed from the Law. Remember, he is again speaking in earthly terms of spiritual things. He says as long as our husband

lives, we cannot be separated or divorced to marry another. But if our husband dies, then we are free to marry another. There it is—your way out—death! All you have to do is die and you are freed from your bad marriage and free to marry another— Christ."

"Death?" Sam exclaimed. "You're starting to lose me. How do you die to live?"

Harry softly smiled. "This is the good news. Christ did it for us. When you believe that Christ died for us, died for our sin, by hanging on that cross, then you died that day also. You ask me how? I don't know. It's a spiritual mystery, but it's true. Jesus did it for us as us, before you and I were born. We were there.

"Once we believe, we are free to enter into a spiritual union with Christ. That is why He is called the bridegroom and the church the bride. We become one with Him. 1 Corinthians 6:17 says, 'But he who is joined to the Lord becomes one spirit with him. One! Not two!"

Harry paused and looked around the room. Silent eyes were glued on Harry. "Any questions ... Sam?"

So there you have it. It's a picture of a spiritual union. It's about the union of the positive (God) to the negative (us). Ever tried to connect two magnets with the same polarity? It doesn't work. What happens when you connect the positive with the negative? The result is a union of the two.

All people are loved by God the same. He is no respecter of persons. And they all have the same choice— to receive the Truth or not. To receive Christ or not. To be married to Christ or not. That is the only issue to be considered, and that is not being talked about. The debate can continue ad infinitum, but the truth of what marriage is really about will never change. It needs no champion.

XIV

BURIED WITH HIM, RAISED WITH HIM

TO ME the ultimate purpose of man is clearly to be the dwelling place of God where He resides in union with our spirit. The Bible is rich in symbolism that tells the same story over and over revealing that mystery which is Christ in us (Col 1:27). For instance, we were recently studying the ordinances in our Bible Study class, baptism and the Lord's Supper. In both I see the same revelation. Let's start with the ordinance of baptism in this article and save the Lord's Supper for another.

First, remember that all symbolism is conveying to us spiritual truths in earthly garb so keep your eyes open. It's not required for salvation but it is symbolic of something that happened. The question beyond the obvious is what?

There are three things depicted in baptism—death, burial, and resurrection. We know it's a picture of what happened to the Christ, but why do we act it out in baptism? Are we going through the motions because we were told to ... to be obedient? Is it simply to remember the sacrifice He made for us? Yes, all these things but it's much more than that.

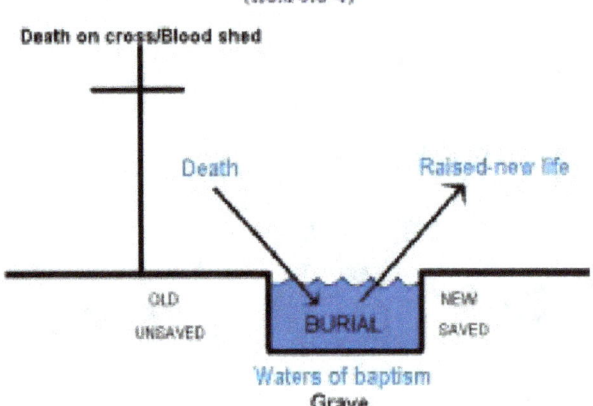

You see when Jesus hung on the cross, so did we! When Jesus died and was buried, so were we. That is what we are showing when we follow Him in baptism. How, you ask? Don't ask me—I don't know. It's just so. That is what the Bible says. Remember, *"I am crucified with Christ?"* (Gal 2:20) It says what it means and means what it says. It may be mystical, but we were there joined spiritually with Christ. We died with Him and we were buried with Him. You could say that Jesus hung there "as us," each one of us individually that believes, yet he took the fall.

What about the resurrection? Were we there for that? Most people stop at the foot of the cross, but it's clear we are meant to be way beyond that if we have eyes to see.

"... [5] even when we were dead in our trespasses, made us alive together with Christ—by grace you have been saved— [6] and raised us up with him and seated us with him in the heavenly places in Christ Jesus, ..." (Eph 2:5-6)

Raised up with him and seated with him in the heavenly places! That's pretty lofty, do you agree? Scripture doesn't stop there.

"For if we have been united with him in a death like his, we shall certainly be united with him in a resurrection like his." (Rom 6:1)

That sums it up. We are showing not only what happened to Christ, but ourselves when we believe.

But that doesn't really answer all the questions. To truly appreciate what Christ did and why we had to join Him in His death, burial, and resurrection we have to see beyond the act to find out what it means spiritually. Why did we have to die as Christ died? Why did we have to join Him in this death, burial, and resurrection?

Paul spells it out how through the law we are freed from the law. Now this is pretty technical. It is for those who know the law.

"For a married woman is bound by law to her husband while he lives, but if her husband dies she is released from the law of marriage, but if her husband dies, she is free from that law ..." (Rom 7:2)

That means she is now free legally to marry another and no longer bound to her previous husband.

So what does that have to do with us? Well, spiritually we have always been in union with and married to another. We were born married to and in union with the not-god, the spirit of Sin. We take on the nature of our Master and it is his desires that we do and they were not good desires. The reason most have a problem believing that is they look back and do not quite see themselves as being *that bad*. You better take a closer look if you don't believe me.

You see, we were never independent persons. That is a delusion. We were always in union with—joined to—a Master, a husband. When Paul says we are slaves either to sin or to righteousness, that is what he is talking about. Our only choice is who that Master is but one thing is for sure, if you don't like the husband you were born with, there is only one way out of that very bad relationship—death! Unlike earthly marriages so easily dissolved, the spiritual laws of marriage and divorce don't work that way. You are bound to that husband as long as he lives. The only way out is death.

As macabre as that sounds, it's not as bad as you think. Christ provided the way. He did it for us. The only thing we have to do is believe. When we believe, we join Him on the cross; we are crucified with Him, die with Him, are buried with Him, and raised with Him. We are now free to marry another, the true bridegroom—Christ. The two of us are now joined together as one.

We are now joined to and one with Christ and we now take on His nature and it is His desires that we do. Praise God for that wonderful act of grace there to be freely received! We are finally free!

XV

THE LORD'S SUPPER

IN THE article, *What is Marriage All About?*, it is clear that marriage refers to our union with Christ. Actually, all scripture points to and confirms our union with Christ if we have eyes to see. The ordinances of Baptism and the Lord's Supper are no exception. In baptism we are united with Christ in his death, burial, and resurrection, truths only spiritually discerned. In this article, we will focus on the second ordinance, the Lord's Supper, which in addition to picturing the sacrifice of Jesus Christ, again symbolizes our union with Him.

The purpose of the Lord's Supper was not necessarily understood in the beginning. In Corinthians, Paul finds the faithful ignorantly desecrating the ordinance and he had to admonish them.

[23] For I received from the Lord what I also delivered to you, that the Lord Jesus on the night when he was betrayed took bread, [24] and when he had given thanks, he broke it, and said, "This is my body which is for you. Do

> *this in remembrance of me."* [25] *In the same way also he took the cup, after supper, saying, "This cup is the new covenant in my blood. Do this, as often as you drink it, in remembrance of me."* [26] *For as often as you eat this bread and drink the cup, you proclaim the Lord's death until he comes.* (1Cor 11:23-26)

There are several things going on here which is the wonderful thing about scripture. It is so rich in meaning and takes so many forms as you view it from various angles. It's about remembrance, sacrifice, death and much more.

First, we know it symbolizes the new covenant and that blood is involved. This macabre picture keeps reappearing over and over from Genesis to Revelation. We saw it in the ordinance of baptism. Why the need for blood and death? Hebrews 9 gives us a clue. It explains that Jesus is the mediator of the new covenant and that a death is needed to redeem us from the transgressions committed under the first covenant. Why? It says that if a will is involved, the death of the one who made it must be established. It cannot take effect as long as the one who made it is alive. Even the first covenant was inaugurated with blood and so must the second, for without the shedding of blood there is no forgiveness of sins. By this shedding of His blood, Christ entered into the holy places not made with hands and into heaven itself to appear in the presence of God on our behalf. This may be foolishness to some, but to us who are being saved it is the power of God. (1 Cor 1:18)

So clearly it is in remembrance of the sacrifice of the Lord's body and the shedding of His blood for our redemption and the forgiveness of sins. But let's not stop there. Why do we symbolically consume his body and his blood? And why do we call it communion?

> *"The cup of blessing which we bless, is it not the communion of the blood of Christ? The bread which we break, is it not the communion of the body of Christ?"* (1Cor 10:1 KJV)

This word, communion, is a very appropriate characterization of what is going on. It means something very intimate ... intercourse ... fellowship ... our union with Christ.

Even before his death on the cross, before the Last Supper, Jesus gave us clues.

> *"[54] Whoever feeds on my flesh and drinks my blood has eternal life, and I will raise him up on the last day. [55] For my flesh is true food, and my blood is true drink. [56] Whoever feeds on my flesh and drinks my blood abides in me, and I in him. [57] As the living Father sent me, and I live because of the Father, so whoever feeds on me, he also will live because of me."* (John 6:54-57)

And:

> *"I am the bread of life; whoever comes to me shall not hunger, and whoever believes in me shall never thirst."*
> (John 6:36)

If you remember many of His disciples took offense and turned back. This was too far out for them. Jesus asked the Twelve if they also wanted to turn back. Peter, in one of his more Spirit filled moments, gave the only answer that made sense—"to whom shall we go? You have the words of eternal life." You have to love that answer.

You see, Jesus was saying that the two of us were to become one. We know we are what we eat. We may find that unfortunately true in our human condition but this is one food that is miraculously wonderful, not to be avoided. It is true food and true drink. This odd illustration of our fleshly union with blood and body of Christ is just another earthly symbol of our spiritual union.

"Whoever feeds on my flesh and drinks my blood abides in me, and I in him." (John 6:56)

It really portrays the ultimate communion given to us.

But he who is joined to the Lord becomes one spirit with him. (1Cor 6:17)

It is just one more way how God makes known how great among the Gentiles are the riches of the glory of this mystery, which is Christ in you, the hope of glory. (Col 1:27 27)

XVI

WATER TO WINE

THE THEME of a recent Bible Study was how to rightly divide the Word of Truth by taking into account the correct literary, historical, and theological context of the Scripture. I found there was no shortage of experts already claiming this ability to properly interpret the Scriptures. There was only one problem—very few of these experts seemed to agree. Interesting.

Of course, there is plenty of information pulled out of context to suit personal interests, both Biblically and secularly. Most of it is propaganda where some faction is trying to influence others. Then there is another type where the individual is trying to persuade himself/herself despite evidence to the contrary. Paul mentions them in his letter to Timothy.

> *³ For the time is coming when people will not endure sound teaching, but having itching ears they will accumulate for themselves teachers to suit their own passions, ⁴ and will turn away from listening to the truth and wander off into myths.(2Tim 4:3-4)*

Setting those aside, then what is the weak link for those that are sincere? I would suggest the theological context. There are plenty of literary and historical experts who can break that down. But unless it is interpreted in the correct theological context, the efforts are for naught.

My theological context is simple. It has to align with God's plan which is:

> *... to make known how great among the Gentiles are the riches of the glory of this mystery, which is Christ in you, the hope of glory. (Col 1:27)*

Take Jesus' first miracle—turning the water into wine. I found no shortage of in-depth analysis. Maybe their points were fine, but they missed the mark. So I'll throw my hat into the ring with what I call the correct interpretation. To refresh you on the story:

> *⁶ Now there were six stone water jars there for the Jewish rites of purification, each holding twenty or thirty gallons. ⁷ Jesus said to the servants, "Fill the jars with water." And they filled them up to the brim. ⁸ And he said to them, "Now draw some out and take it to the master of the feast." So they took it. ⁹ When the master of the feast tasted the water now become wine, and did not know where it came from (though the servants who had drawn the water knew), the master of the feast called the*

bridegroom [10] and said to him, "Everyone serves the good wine first, and when people have drunk freely, then the poor wine. But you have kept the good wine until now." [11] This, the first of his signs, Jesus did at Cana in Galilee, and manifested his glory. And his disciples believed in him. (John 2:6-11)

We have the literary context—it was a wedding and they were out of wine. We have the historical context—weddings went on for a week and running out of wine for your guests was, well ... a really bad thing. What about the theological context? Let me break it down quickly and simply.

The stone water jars represent us. The number six represents the number of man. The Bible is rife with images and metaphors referring to men as vessels, jars, pots, temple, etc. Sorry to offend those *vessels* that think they are something more, but the fact is that is all we are—vessels to contain something. The question is contain what? Simply stated, it's a person.

To start with, we contain the false god represented by the plain water. This person is the sin spirit we are all born with and we take on the nature (taste) of what fills us. That is why we sin.

When Jesus turned the water into wine, in one fell swoop he pictured God's entire plan—how He would replace the sin spirit with His own through His death, burial, and resurrection.

Voila! The water turned into wine, the symbol of God's Holy Spirit filling our created spirit.

Now we can say:

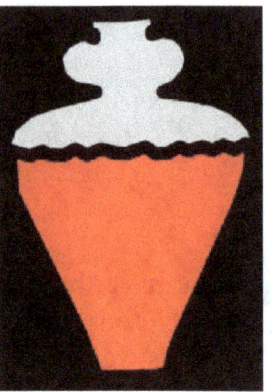

But we have this treasure in jars of clay, to show that the surpassing power belongs to God and not to us. (2Cor 4:7)

Which is Christ in us, the mystery unveiled! When he says, "... the surpassing power belongs to God and not to us," that removes any trace of self-righteousness or self-effort. He did it all.

You see, we don't now and never did have any power to be righteous or *good*. We are simply faced with a choice of whom to contain. And we take on the nature of whom we contain—either the false god or the true God. That should take away any false condemnation or any false pride in us. Notice the stone water jars are still the stone water jars. They didn't change. The contents changed. It's the same with us.

The vessels are made out of many different kinds of materials to make up the body of Christ serving different functions. Some may not be as pretty by worldly standards as others but we all play the same role in God's plan, to contain Him.

[19] Or do you not know that your body is a temple of the Holy Spirit within you, whom you have from God? You are not your own, [20] for you were bought with a price. So glorify God in your body. (1Cor 6:19-20)

XVII

PASSOVER
A SPIRITUAL ALLEGORY

MANY FIND the stories in the Old Testament interesting and others boring and difficult to digest. To the uninitiated, not much is seen beyond the historical perspective. True, they are actual events, but if viewed solely as a history lesson, the real point could easily be missed. Jesus considered them to be much more than historical.

You search the Scriptures because you think that in them you have eternal life; and it is they that bear witness about me, (John 5:39)

That is interesting because I don't recall Him being mentioned by name in the Old Testament. Where and how is it that these stories bear witness of the coming Messiah? It may not always obvious, but it is there if you know where to look. The only way to properly interpret scripture is to consider the dual meaning, which in all cases is a spiritual one, usually a spiritual allegory. They are two sides of the same coin.

Exodus is rich in spiritual allegory and Passover is the most important one. The Israelites were in Egypt 430 years, most of which were in bondage to the Egyptians. They cried out to the Lord and He heard them. He sent Moses to Pharaoh to ask Pharaoh to release His people. Pharaoh refused. After nine plagues, Pharaoh's heart was still hardened and still he would not let the people go. God had one last card to play, a far-reaching one that was His plan all along. This last epic event would bring Pharaoh to his knees and provide mankind with the blueprint for both salvation and judgment, a choice that must be made by everyone on earth. God would pass judgment on Egypt and its idols. He would pass through the land killing the firstborn of man and beast. But He provided a way for the elect—the Israelites—to avoid the wrath to come if the people would follow in faith the specific instructions given to them through Moses.

Most people know the basics of Passover. They were to take a lamb, kill it, put the blood of the lamb on the lintels and doorposts of their homes and eat it with unleavened bread and bitter herbs. When the destroyer came, he would see the blood and pass over them as he executed judgment. The Israelites were to eat the Passover with sandals on their feet and girded with a staff in their hand. In other words, they were to be saddled up and ready to go. Whatever was going to happen was going to happen fast.

The best way to understand the story is to visualize Israel as one person. God refers to Israel as His first born son (Ex 4:22). It is also the story of every man (and woman).

The first question is why does God take such a special interest in Israel? Were they better, were they more righteous? The answer is no. They were pagans just like the rest of us. They worshipped the gods of Egypt just like they are worshipped today. An idol is anything that is put in front of or in place of God—anything that separates us from the love of God. They are not figurines or golden calves. Those are just symbols of idolatry.

The reason God heard the Israelites is solely because of the Promise He made to Abraham, Isaac, and Jacob. God's gifts and calling are irrevocable (Rom 11:29). It is because of the principle of election. Nothing more.

If so, why did God wait so many years to redeem them from slavery? We know He is not slack concerning His promises.

The Lord is not slow to fulfill his promise as some count slowness, but is patient toward you,[1] not wishing that any should perish, but that all should reach repentance.
(2Pet 3:9)

The answer is the Israelites were not ready. Their bondage in Egypt is a picture of every man's bondage to sin, the Adamic nature we were born with, a consequence of the choices made in the garden. God left them there so they would taste to the dregs the bitterness of this bondage and finally realize that they had no power of their own to extricate themselves, to save themselves. No matter how hard we struggle and squirm, sin is like quicksand. The more we fight it, the deeper we sink. We have to come to the realization we cannot save ourselves. There has to be another way. The bitter herbs were to remind us of the bitterness of that slavery.

The households were to purge their houses of leaven. Leaven has additional meanings. It represents sin in our lives. They were to repent, to purge themselves of their idolatry before they would be able to leave. Anyone who ate anything with leaven would be cut off.

The lamb is the most important symbol of all. It was to be roasted, entirely consumed, and not a bone was to be broken. It is symbolic because it had no power to actually remove sin just like the entire sacrificial system had no real power to remove sin. This was evident when Israel was in the wilderness. More than once they would have lopped Moses' head off and returned to their previous state. They carried that sin nature with them.

No, there had to be more to it. The lamb and the blood of the lamb pointed forward to the coming of the Messiah, the true Lamb of God that would take sin away. When John the Baptist saw Jesus approaching, he testified that He was that Lamb of God. By the way, John was not a Baptist. He was a Jew.

The next day he saw Jesus coming toward him, and said, "Behold, the Lamb of God, who takes away the sin of the world! (John 1:29)

Passover showed the way that God would provide years later by entering the world in the form of man as His only begotten Son. Jesus was the sacrifice that poured out his life for all mankind to truly save us from sin and the wages of sin.

⁸ but God shows his love for us in that while we were still sinners, Christ died for us.⁹ Since, therefore, we have now been justified by his blood, much more shall we be saved by him from the wrath of God. (Rom 5:8-9)

For those who believe in the Son of Man, they are covered by the blood in the sight of God. When judgment comes at the end of the age, He will see the blood. *When He sees the blood, He will pass over.*

Why don't Christians observe Passover? Well, they could I suppose, but they observe a different ordinance now—The Lord's Supper. What Passover pointed to has been fulfilled by Christ. It is no coincidence that Easter and Passover are celebrated close to one another. What we call the Last Supper was actually the Last Passover Supper that Christ celebrated with His disciples. This all occurred during Passover for a reason. He was the Passover. The new ordinance represents the new covenant in His blood. It symbolizes Him pouring out his life for us and us consuming the Lamb of God in His body and His blood:

> *^{26} Now as they were eating, Jesus took bread, and after blessing it broke it and gave it to the disciples, and said, "Take, eat; this is my body." ^{27} And he took a cup, and when he had given thanks he gave it to them, saying, "Drink of it, all of you, ^{28} for this is my blood of the covenant, which is poured out for many for the forgiveness of sins. ^{29} I tell you I will not drink again of this fruit of the vine until that day when I drink it new with you in my Father's kingdom."* (Matt 26:26-29)

God had to provide a way. We cannot save ourselves. And He did. In Christ.

XVIII

CAN YOU FLY?

HAVE YOU ever wondered if there was something wrong with you? You wanted to go right but somehow you ended up going left? You wanted to do good but somehow ... well ... it didn't quite work out the way you planned? You might have even wondered if you were possessed.

That's good if you have felt that way. Now I know you think I'm nuts, but bear with me. First of all, you need to know there is nothing wrong with you. God didn't make any mistakes. You are perfectly made but there is a slight problem. The problem is we aren't made to be good. Even Jesus said, *"Why callest thou me good? There is none good but God."* (Mark 10:18 KJV)

Was he being facetious or was he trying to tell us something about how we are made? I am going to use a true story to illustrate my point. This happened to me and it is recounted in this edited excerpt from *The Lost Coin*, a novel I wrote in 2015.

To set the stage, Sam Season is a student pilot who just received his solo certificate and is going up for the first time by himself to practice some maneuvers. It's a perfect day. The plane is in perfect condition. But something goes horribly wrong. Let's pick it up in Chapter 1. Sam is at altitude and practicing:

Sam started out with some easy maneuvers keeping his eye on the airport. He liked to leave breadcrumbs of landmarks to make it easier to navigate back. He practiced the usual maneuvers, banking to the right, banking to the left. This was very routine and after a while he was a little bored. Need to spice this up, he thought.

He decided to practice a power take-off stall. This was more interesting and required some real skill. It was done to simulate a stall on take-off and how to recover. One of the first things Sam learned was that an aeronautical stall had nothing to do with stalling the engine. A stall means the airplane has no lift. There is a minimum airspeed required to keep a plane aloft. Anything less, the plane falls. There is no gradual loss of lift. It was all or none. When a plane stalled, it fell from the sky like a rock.

He pulled the nose up, thrust the throttle all the way back in and reset the trim to take-off position. He inched the nose up, slowly, watching the speed drop off and keeping his eye on the little white ball on the lower left hand side of the dash. That indicated that enough right rudder was being employed to compensate for the torque of the engine and keep it level. As the plane speed slowed, more and more rudder was applied to keep the ball in the center. He waited apprehensively for the plane to stall which would be a quick dip of the nose if he did it correctly from which he would nose the plane down to recover enough airspeed to resume control.

Slowly ... slowly, he nosed the plane upward. Slowly the airspeed dropped. The ball stayed centered. As he approached 40 knots, he knew he was getting close to stall speed. The right rudder was pushed to the floorboard. And then the stall. The nose dropped. He pushed the stick forward and quickly recovered, level and flying straight. He was proud of himself. It was textbook.

Suddenly without warning and with full power still employed, the plane dropped. It fell like a rock. No lift. The strings cut. No control. Straight down with full throttle. The plane went into an immediate counterclockwise spin. The earth rose up to meet him, a kaleidoscope of greens, oranges, and browns in a dizzying blur.

Sam immediately reacted. His instructor had shown him how to recover but he had never done it himself. He struggled to remember.

How did he do it again? He panicked. The altimeter was spinning, only 2,000 feet left to recover. Full right rudder to stop the spin? ... yes ... that's it.

Sam pushed the right rudder to the floorboard. No effect. The plane continued to spin out of control as the rotating earth loomed larger and larger. He pulled on the elevators. Hard. As hard as he could. No effect. They would not budge. He turned the ailerons clockwise hard. The plane continued its downward spin. He was out of ideas. Totally helpless.

The situation was dire with only seconds remaining and he knew it. The tach was redlined. The airspeed was pegged. In the few seconds left, Sam's life started passing before him.

The plane seemed to spiral downward at supersonic speed. The earth roared up to meet it. He never thought about praying nor had he time. He resigned himself to his fate as he twisted and pulled on the controls. What else could he do?

Not to be a spoiler, but Sam does survive (besides, you know I'm alive). He is hesitant to continue his flying but his instructor convinces him to go up with him one more time just to show him what he did wrong. We pick it back up in Chapter 7. George Sherman is giving Sam instructions:

"Ok. Easy does it. This time we are going to do a power take-off stall, just like you did before, only we are not going to try and recover. We are going to let it stall and go into a nose dive."

"Okayyyy, you're the boss." Sam set the trim to takeoff and nosed the plane up and up. The plane slowed more and more as Sam increased the attitude. Images of his last flight flooded back to him. His stomach knotted up. He kept the little white ball in the middle with the right rudder. He could feel in his bones what was about to happen. Suddenly the nose dropped. As instructed, Sam did not try to recover. He let it fall. It nosed straight down and started to spin. Déjà vu.

George touched Sam's tense shoulder. "It's ok, Sam," he said pointing his finger at the throttle, "pull the throttle all the way back."

Sam wasted no time yanking it to idle.

"Now, don't touch anything," Sherm instructed. "Give it a little right rudder and keep your hands on the stick to guide it."

The plane stopped spinning and began to level off on its own without any effort. Sam looked over at Sherm. He was shocked.

"Really!" Sam almost shouted as he reset the trim and gave it some gas. "You mean that was all there was to it? This thing flies itself?"

Sherm just smiled. "Almost, Sam. Look, what happened that day was not your fault. You didn't have the proper training. That's my fault. The fact that you recovered is nothing short of a miracle but you did it. Let me explain what you did. First of all, this plane is designed to fly. It's a natural flyer. The only way it can't fly is if we make it not fly."

"Make it not fly?" Sam asked puzzled.

"Exactly. It was born to fly. That's what it does naturally. All it needs is some guidance. When you kept the throttle in and were pulling on the controls, you were in effect holding it in a stall, preventing it from flying. If you had taken your hands off all the controls, it probably would have done what comes naturally—flying.

"Amazing," Sam said. "All along I thought I was flying the plane and lo and behold, I wasn't flying it at all. It was flying itself. You're saying all I have to do is make small adjustments and point it in the right direction."

"That's about it. The plane is going to follow the laws of aerodynamics if the operator aligns himself with them. If he fights them, it doesn't work. The only thing I can figure out about what saved you, other than divine intervention, was that when you turned the ailerons in the direction of the spin, at least you stopped fighting it. That was apparently enough alignment to come out of the spin into that spiral you described and defeat death."

Agree with your adversary quickly in the way came to Sam's mind as Sherm talked. He kept mulling over what he had just learned. It was such a simple concept.

Simple? That was a term he and Mo had been discussing a lot of recently. Sometimes it was too simple to see.

So then this light bulb goes off in Sam's head. He suddenly realizes that what happened in the air is analogous to the failures in his life. He excitedly explains it to his girlfriend, Mo. We pick it up at the end of Chapter 7:

"What I learned today is there are not just immutable laws of physics in the universe, there are immutable spiritual laws. You can fight them if you want, but they always win. Take the plane as a metaphor. Say I am the plane. The cockpit is my spirit. It's perfectly made, designed to do what it does, just as man is. There is nothing wrong with it. How it operates is determined by the pilot. The pilot knows what he is doing and guides the plane according to his will. When aligned with all the laws of aerodynamics there is no problem. But if it's not aligned with those laws, it falls from the sky. If our cockpit contains God and we are in alignment with His will, everything works perfectly. If not—disaster. Anytime the plane decides it can fly itself, or we decide to climb into the cockpit ourselves, God lets us so we can prove to ourselves it can't be done. If we take over for the pilot acting in the delusion of independence against the laws of nature, the result is always the same. We crash and burn. The plane is just the vessel, the container in need of a pilot. Man is just the vessel, the container in need of an operator. In my case, in my ignorance, I took a perfectly good vessel and forced it into a stall until it all but killed me. We do the same thing in our spiritual lives. When we take control and start jerking and pulling at the controls because we can't wait on God, we force ourselves into a spiritual stall. Wait, the Bible says, on the Lord."

What Sam learned was that we are all perfectly made vessels, but that is all we are. It is a delusion propagated by Satan, who believes it himself, that we operate ourselves as independent persons. We are referred to as jars or vessels in the Bible. Our spirit is the container. The one we contain is in control, either God or the not-god, and we take on the nature of whomever that is, either good or evil. There is no co-pilot. If you think you can do a better job, that you can pilot or co-pilot, He will let you work at it until you finally wear yourself out.

So if you want to fly, stop fiddling with the knobs and let the Pilot do his job and fly His perfectly made vessel. Now that certainly makes my yoke easy and my burden light knowing that the only one who is good is God and I no longer have to try or pretend to be something I am not. I just manifest the Christ in me and His goodness.

XIX

DO YOU HATE HYPOCRITES?

TELL ME, what do you think of hypocrites? Ever hear someone say, "Oh, how I hate those self-righteous hypocrites" often in reference to Christians? Are you one of them? If so, it might tell a lot about you.

Here is the problem. Right then and there you just witnessed a self-righteous act of hypocrisy. Because if they can't stand hypocrites, how do they stand in front of a mirror each morning and shave or put on your makeup? How do you stand yourself? There is not one of us that either is or has not been a hypocrite.

"What?" you say. "How dare you put me in that category? I am not a hypocrite!"

Really? Well, let's examine a few things. Let's start with the definition. A hypocrite is *"a person who puts on a false appearance of virtue or religion or a person who acts in contradiction to his or her stated beliefs or feelings."*

So, without a doubt, we just trapped a lot of *religious* people. In fact, Jesus found this one particular group the worst offenders. He harshly condemned the religious leaders of the day as hypocrites:

> *"Woe to you, scribes and Pharisees, hypocrites! For you are like whitewashed tombs, which outwardly appear beautiful, but within are full of dead people's bones and all uncleanness."* (Matt 23:27)

Okay. We have that group covered. You may actually know a religious hypocrite or two. Whether they practice what they say or not, that doesn't make the gospel any less true. Let's move on. There is more. We don't want to leave anyone out.

"What does that have to do with me?" you ask. "I don't even believe in all that religious, hypocritical mumbo jumbo let alone practice it."

Now you are digging a deeper hole. Because as soon as you say these people are hypocrites, that their beliefs are fairy tales, you just replaced theirs with your own. Once you do that, then you too will be held accountable for what you preach and whether you adhere to your own made up principles. You might just want to examine your own beliefs because if they are not based on truth then they are just a figment of your imagination. You made them up. That is a scary thing, but it doesn't stop people from preaching made up gospels particularly with the ease of social media platforms like Facebook and Twitter.

"Preach? What gospel?" you ask. "I'm not preaching any gospel!"

Oh yes you are. Just look at Facebook, Twitter, and the not so hidden agendas of the conventional media and political platforms. There is no shortage of self-righteous sermons that all have the same basis: "if only everyone would think like me, this world would be so much better off. If they would only be as loving as me, if they would only be as unselfish as me, what a wonderful world this would be." They preach their personal ideologies under the pretense of love and guess what? If you don't agree, just watch the pitchforks of hate come out and attack the non-believers.

What did Jesus say? "Hypocrites!" Welcome to the party fellow hypocrites!

You hypocrite, first take the log out of your own eye, and then you will see clearly to take the speck out of your brother's eye. (Matt 7:5)

So let me tell you how to get out of this quagmire that is your personal hypocrisy of self-righteousness. You see, our gospel is true and it is fact based. If you want to compare yourself to the failings of the faithful, or the unfaithful as the case may be, then you have just indicted yourself. Your measuring stick is way out of calibration.

Ever hear someone say, "I'm as good as he/she is?" Of course you have. And therein lays the problem. Because they are right. He or she is as good as me or anyone else. But I'm a sinner. I admit it. The only difference is I am a sinner saved by grace. Everyone that denies they are a sinner is a true hypocrite. All of us have been there, all of us have been hypocrites, because all have sinned and come short of the glory of God. (Rom 3:23)

Until you come to that conclusion about yourself, you might want to be less concerned and judgmental about the "other" hypocrites and consider the truth about yourself. At the end of the age, you won't have anyone to point at and say, "What about them?" They won't be there. Why? Well ...

There is therefore now no condemnation for those who are in Christ Jesus. (Rom 8:1)

I don't know about you, but I like that—a lot. Freeing oneself from the hypocrisy of self-righteousness is so easy and available to all. Just believe on the Lord Jesus Christ and His righteousness, not your own:

[9] ..., if you confess with your mouth that Jesus is Lord and believe in your heart that God raised him from the dead, you will be saved. [10] For with the heart one believes and is justified, and with the mouth one confesses and is saved. (Rom 10:9-10)

Amen!

XX

THE FEAR OF THE LORD

The fear of the Lord is the beginning of knowledge; fools despise wisdom and instruction.
(Prov 1:7)

MANY CHRISTIANS struggle with reconciling the fact that we are commanded to "love God with all our heart and with all our soul and with all our might" (Deut 6:5) while at the same time being told to fear Him. Why would we fear someone we love?

To soften it a little bit, the word yirȧh in the OT also means to be in awe, to reverence and respect. But being ordered to love, fear and respect a person seems cold, sterile, and narcissistic. And if it is something that has to be dredged up or coerced, then it is most likely untrue. Clouds and wind with no rain. Jesus warns of fraudulent love and respect.

> [22] *On that day many will say to me, 'Lord, Lord, did we not prophesy in your name, and cast out demons in your name, and do many mighty works in your name?'* [23] *And then will I declare to them, 'I never knew you; depart from me, you workers of lawlessness.'* (Matt 7:22-23)

So simply saying you fear God or love God doesn't get it. It doesn't make it true. That creates a dilemma. When do we know that we love and fear God ... that it is real ... and that it is enough? And what about the contradistinction? Love and fear are contradictory, a dichotomy that is difficult to square in the same sentence.

Or are they? God has a funny way of making seeming polar opposites dwell together in a congruent union that totally defies human logic. He loves doing that.

If we consider only the letter, the words seem cold and set us at arm's distance from God. Maybe you had an earthly father that you loved and respected yet found he was not approachable. Yet that is impossible with God. Scripture is clear that God is Love (1 John 4:8). Pure Love! He is someone that is standing right in front of us with open arms, ready to love us, to scoop us up and heal all our scars and hurts. Something needs to be added. It's called Spirit and without it, the letter is dead.

> *... who has made us sufficient to be ministers of a new covenant, not of the letter but of the Spirit. For the letter kills, but the Spirit gives life.* (3Cor 3:6)

So if God is Love, where did all this fear come from? Well, we have to go back to the beginning ... to Adam. What really happened in the Garden? Adam and Eve were living a "give no thought" to life or tomorrow, bebopping through the forest buck naked and happy. It was normal and natural. Then they ate of the Tree of the Knowledge of Good and Evil and immediately their eyes were opened. All of a sudden they were ashamed. They were naked ... exposed!

Then what happened? Did God abandon them because they had disobeyed? Did He hide Himself from them? The answer is no. He came to them in the garden in love just like he always had. It was Adam and Eve who hid.

⁹ But the Lord God called to the man and said to him, "Where are you?" ¹⁰ And he said, "I heard the sound of you in the garden, and I was afraid, because I was naked, and I hid myself." (Gen 3:9-10)

Where did that come from? Something changed. All of a sudden he was afraid. He was self-conscious. God didn't hide. He did!

I remember my Mom asking my Dad one time, "How come we never sit next to each other anymore when we go for a drive?" (for those of you old enough to remember the ubiquitous bench seats)

"I haven't moved," he replied dryly and matter of factly.

Hmmm ... interesting. God hasn't changed. He hasn't moved. He is the same yesterday and today and forever. He never stopped loving Adam and Eve. He came to them ... in love. They hid. They moved away from God. God didn't come to punish them. He simply explained the consequences of their decision and to tell them He had a plan to turn them back so they could return to Him.

The fear they experienced was purely irrational, viewed now through their distorted lens. Until they returned, all they would see is a God full of wrath ...

someone to fear. But the truth is the wrath of God, which is the opposite of His nature that is Love, was their (and our) personal choice to accept by rejecting Him. They traded one in for the other.

Whoever believes in the Son has eternal life; whoever does not obey the Son shall not see life, but the wrath of God remains on him. (John 3:36)

So it is no mystery that the world in general sees God as a God of wrath. Without the Spirit, they see a cold and judgmental God. But that is not for you. You have the Spirit. The wrath of God does not rest on you or in you because you are in Christ. That is the mystery hidden from the ages but now revealed to you.

To them God chose to make known how great among the Gentiles are the riches of the glory of this mystery, which is Christ in you, the hope of glory. (Col 1:27)

The fear of the Lord may be the jumping off point, but it no longer has a place in those who are in Christ.

Despite knowing this truth, many Christians still have an unhealthy fear of God. They fear He is going to do something to them ... to hurt them ... to take something away from them. They fear He is going to punish them for not loving Him enough, or loving something or someone else too much, or for some sin they struggle with. Their joy is eaten up like a cancer, the negative swallowing up the positive in total contradiction to who God is. The positive is always meant to swallow up the negative. Not the other way around. Any other view is looking through the wrong end of the telescope.

Does the Lord send trials and tribulations? Yes ... but not to hurt... not to make us afraid. It is all done in love because that is who He is. It is impossible for Him to act contrary to His nature. It is because He loves you and wants to bring you to a mature faith that is perfect, lacking nothing.

> *² Count it all joy, my brothers, when you meet trials of various kinds, ³ for you know that the testing of your faith produces steadfastness. ⁴ And let steadfastness have its full effect, that you may be perfect and complete, lacking in nothing.* (James 1:24)

And what about loving Him enough? In Christ, we never have to worry about a lack of love and reverence for God. You can't put a cork in it if you tried. Think about it. If you stand on the pinnacle of a mountain or on the floor of a river valley, on the edge of the Grand Canyon, experience the miracle of birth, immerse yourself in your favorite music, or just consider we live on a beautiful planet whirling through space without a net, then the awe and love just flows out of us spontaneously, like ... well you know:

> *³⁸ Whoever believes in me, as the Scripture has said, 'Out of his heart will flow rivers of living water.'" ³⁹ Now this he said about the Spirit, whom those who believed in him were to receive ...* (John 7:38-39)

Be anxious for nothing. Know that "God loves you" and it is not simply another trite expression. It is more real than anything you can imagine.

Amen.

XXI

IS GUN CONTROL THE ANSWER?

ANOTHER WAVE of mass shootings is echoed by another hollow sounding wave of righteous rhetoric that plays like a worn out record. The self-righteous left meets the equally righteous indignation of the right who will defend the mother lode of guns to the last man (or woman). Not to worry gun lovers. Rhetoric by definition does not require an answer and this will be no different thanks to a completely dysfunctional legislative system. The existing laws are ridiculous but even if more were passed, they would be unenforceable and all the grandfathered guns out there now will keep us armed to the teeth for generations. As far as sociopaths or criminally insane, just like you will always have the poor, they aren't going anywhere soon either.

The fact that there are so many guns in this country does affect the murder rate which for a western civilization should be embarrassing. And it is ridiculous that there is so much access to weapons that have no use other than to fight a war. If there is a threat, foreign or domestic, that our armed forces can't handle, then those for complete access can certainly say they told us so.

In all deference to the victims and their families, the rhetoric is clouds and wind with no rain because it wants to deal with symptoms and not the root cause. So what is the root cause? Not many want to discuss that. That might be even more embarrassing and hit close to home. One politician says, "Stuff happens." Hmmmm. Maybe right, but he could have worded it differently than a bumper sticker. Another says it's because of sin and evil in the world. Now we are getting close.

I'm not sure what the murder weapon of choice was for Cain, our very first murderer. I guess we could have banned sticks and stones right then and stemmed the tide. However, two of the three little pigs' houses would have been classified as deadly weapons.

But it wasn't the abundance of sticks or stones that killed righteous Able. To be blunt, it was Satan (Sin) operating in the person of Cain to bring into fruition the first murderous act and was nothing more than an expression of who he was.

You are of your father the devil, and your will is to do your father's desires. He was a murderer from the beginning, and does not stand in the truth, because there is no truth in him. When he lies, he speaks out of his own character, for he is a liar and the father of lies. (John 8:44)`

You see, this is the dark secret no one wants to talk about. Though we may not be *as bad* as murderers, it shines a bright light that comes uncomfortably close to all of us threatening to expose secrets we work very hard to conceal behind the façade of civility. It blows all that self-righteousness to hell and there is no way we are going voluntarily reveal ourselves for what we are. No, we are going to buff that shiny facade of ourselves in a dark room and project how good we are, not how bad. Nevertheless, you can't argue with the truth.

> *... for all have sinned and fall short of the glory of God, ... (Rom 3:23)*

"Well, if you are so smart," you ask, "what is the answer?" Good question.

The simple answer is Christ. The only way to eradicate sin is to replace it with Christ. That is what Ezekiel was talking about.

> *^{26} And I will give you a new heart, and a new spirit I will put within you. And I will remove the heart of stone from your flesh and give you a heart of flesh. ^{27} And I will put my Spirit within you, and cause you to walk in my statutes and be careful to obey my rules. (Ezekiel 36:26-27)*

The sin nature, controlled by Satan, is replaced with the Love Nature which is Christ, but only for those who believe. We go from:

> *Among whom also we all had our conversation in times past in the lusts of our flesh, fulfilling the desires of the flesh and of the mind; and were by nature the children of wrath, even as others. (Eph 2:3)*

To:

> *Whereby are given unto us exceeding great and precious promises: that by these ye might be partakers of the*

divine nature, having escaped the corruption that is in the world through lust ... (2Pet 1:4)

Now for the part you won't like. Not all are going to come to Christ. They are going to stay in the closet and deny that they also are in need of a savior. They will continue to believe in their own self-righteousness and that they can legislate morality, sidestepping the issue. History proves this wrong. They can restrain, and only for a while, but they cannot eradicate.

Of course, the classic question always comes up. If God is so good, why does He allow all this death and destruction? He does it out of love which may sound contradictory, but it's true. He created man in His image, the most striking likeness being our ability to choose. He could pluck those off the earth at any time that choose self over God, but His work is not done. He has many more people on earth now and yet to come that will receive His kingdom. Until then, we all will have to live with the consequences. Stuff will continue to happen.

XXII

FAITH OR WORKS?

I USED to have a little anxiety after reading James' narrative about faith and works. He doesn't pull any punches. "Faith without works is dead," he says starkly. "Be doers of the word, not just hearers." He goes even further and cites how Abraham was justified by works when he offered up his son Isaac on the alter.

Now I'm even more perplexed. Justified by works? I never saw that one coming. Doesn't that fly in the face of everything we have had drilled into us? Doesn't Ephesians tell us we are saved by grace, not of works, lest any should boast? Which is it? Faith or works? Can't we ever get it straight?

I immediately start to look at myself and question if I have either. Do I have enough faith? Am I doing enough? I start looking for results and begin to tally up what I have. I compare them to the great works of others. Do mine make the grade? I sink into despair as the evil of uncertainty creeps into my soul.

What is the answer? These two things are seemingly contradictory, but we know that cannot be. They must be one. The word of God has to be seamless or it is not true.

One thing is for sure, focusing on results is a slippery slope. Even Jesus said things that were seemingly contradictory. Do you remember what he said to the righteous?

> *^{34} Then the King will say to those on his right, 'Come, you who are blessed by my Father, inherit the kingdom prepared for you from the foundation of the world. ^{35} For I was hungry and you gave me food, I was thirsty and you gave me drink, I was a stranger and you welcomed me,*
> *(Matt 25:34-35)*

And their surprised response?

> *^{37} Then the righteous will answer him, saying, 'Lord, when did we see you hungry and feed you, or thirsty and give you drink?'* *(Matt 25:37)*

What is this? You didn't know, you righteous person? How did that happen? Were your works so unnoticed that no one counted them for righteousness, including yourself. Were you lamenting all that time "woe is us" as we compared ourselves to others? You can't judge by appearances, can you? Judge a righteous judgment.

And do you remember what the Lord said to the proud and arrogant so certain of their good works?

> *^{22} On that day many will say to me, 'Lord, Lord, did we not prophesy in your name, and cast out demons in your name, and do many mighty works in your name?' ^{23} And*

then will I declare to them, 'I never knew you; depart from me, you workers of lawlessness.' (Matt 7:22-23)

Wow! Who saw that coming either? All these great and wonderful works burning up before their eyes as they left, no doubt cursing God. You can't judge by appearances, can you? Judge a righteous judgment.

Focusing on results is an evil condition. By doing so, the simple are filled up with pride while the weaker ones are deceived into doubting themselves, even their salvation.

So, back to the question—what is the answer? Well, for sure they are one thing. They have to be. You have to look at the vantage point of James who is flying at a much higher level than most of us. In his mind, there is no disconnect between the two. They are one and the same, joined together, two sides of the same coin. He said Abraham was justified by his works but at the same time said that Abraham believed God and that was counted to him as righteousness. That is why he says,

But someone will say, "You have faith and I have works." Show me your faith apart from your works, and I will show you my faith by my works. (James 2:18)

One cannot exist without the other if we are in Christ. It is because of the Vine–Branch relationship. The works are the fruit of who we are in Christ. Because we are one with Him, He manifests Himself through us, as us. If we forget that and step back into the delusion of being separate from God, the delusion of independence, we are on our own and the works that we do are no longer His. Any works based on self-effort will burn. But if we abide in Him, the fruit is a naturally occurring fruit, a lasting fruit. He works the works Himself, in us, as us. No effort.

Remember what Jesus said you had to do, to do the works of God?

^{28} Then they said to him, "What must we do, to be doing the works of God?" ^{29} Jesus answered them, "This is the work of God, that you believe in him whom he has sent." (John 6:28-29)

That's all! Believe! Don't look for results. You will be disappointed. It's not you! It's Christ! He does the works.

I am crucified with Christ: nevertheless I live; yet not I, but Christ liveth in me: and the life which I now live in the flesh I live by the faith of the Son of God, who loved me, and gave himself for me. (Gal 2:20)

I no longer live. He lives! In me! As me! He does the works! Believe!!!!!!!!!

XXIII

FAITH OR POSITIVE THINKING?

"I PREFER to be positive." You have heard this out of the mouths of many. Positive thinking has been around a long time, popularized by Norman Vincent Peale. It sounds good and, I think, many consider it the same thing as or at least akin to what we call faith. But is it really? Most of its adherents have faith in nothing other than themselves.

According to one source, positive thinking is a "technique" for changing your attitude and fostering optimism. It is a mental attitude in which you expect good and favorable results. Another says positive thinking is the process of creating thoughts that create and transform energy into reality. To sum it up, they say that you, and you alone, by the power of your sheer will, are able to convert the lemons thrown at you into lemonade.

The definition of faith on the other hand is on the lips of most Christians who know this verse by heart:

> *Now faith is the assurance of things hoped for, the conviction of things not seen.* (Heb. 11:1)

The difference may seem subtle, but the gap between them is as far as the east is from the west. They are two different things altogether. Positive thinking is simply another form of negative thinking masquerading around as an efficacious replacement for faith. It tries to replicate something that only God has the power to do. It has the appearance of godliness but denies its power (2 Tim 3:5). This is why.

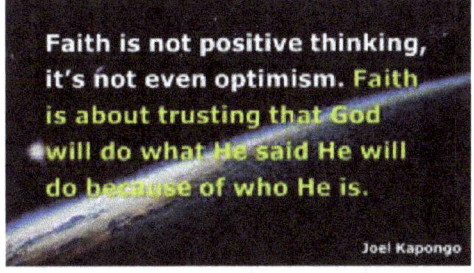

The "Positive Thinker" makes a conscious decision to take some situation in their lives with the potential to affect them adversely and think about it in a positive light. By doing so, they have just admitted, acknowledged, and accepted the fact that there is a problem which, according to Webster, is a matter or situation regarded as unwelcome or harmful and needing to be dealt with and overcome. The fact that they have decided to *pretend* this negative situation does not exist does not make it go away. It gives it life. You can put lipstick on a pig, but all you end up with is pretty pig.

Faith operates from a totally different perspective. Its source is from the inside-out; the opposite of the outside-in of positive thinking. It is not a conscious effort to view something as good. Faith knows that everything is good, even things that have the so-called appearance of evil. Now this is a tall glass of water to drink, even for most Christians who have a divided outlook. Let's check it out with a few verses.

I form light and create darkness; I make well-being and create calamity; I am the Lord, who does all these things. (Isa 45:7)

This says there is only one power in the universe. That is God's power. Only He can do all these things. But we know that He cannot do anything except out of who He is. Since God is Love (1 John 4:8), then everything—not just what we perceive as good things—is out of Love and it is good. Remember what He said in the beginning?

And God saw everything that he had made, and behold, it was very good. (Gen 1:31)

God said that everything was good. Well, nothing has changed except for man's new divided consciousness, now knowing good and evil. God never took that back. And if everything is good, then we can believe that this is true:

And we know that for those who love God all things work together for good, for those who are called according to his purpose. (Rom 8:28)

And if that is true, then we *KNOW* and have assurance that all things will work out according to God's purpose which is *ALWAYS* good, despite appearances. Knowing means we don't have to put any effort into believing it. It just is. The positive thinker has to support their decision with effort. That takes energy which at some point gives out. Faith streams like rivers of living water and has the Son of God as its infinite supply.

The interesting thing is that both may have the same outcome. The positive thinker may delude him or herself into believing they worked the problem out on their own, but God says different:

The heart of man plans his way, but the Lord establishes his steps. (Prov 8:28)

They can claim credit, but there was never a moment when God was not in control. Whether we *see* Him in each situation or not, He *is* there, working everything according to His will.

Jesus said, "Which of you by taking thought can add one cubit unto his stature (Matt 6:27)?" It all happens the same way whether you think about it, fuss about it, fume about it, plan it, conspire or just believe. The latter is much easier.

Jesus said, "The light of the body is the eye: if therefore thine eye be single, thy whole body shall be full of light (Matt 6:22 KJV)." Stop believing in two powers, one good and one evil. There is only *ONE* power. Do not judge by appearances and turn into a pillar of salt. Remember that God said, "I will never leave you nor forsake you (Deut 31:6)." Just believe and find rest for your souls.

XXIV

WHY BOTHER PRAYING?

IN A recent Bible Study class on prayer, it was no time before the question was asked, "Why do we pray?" The insinuation is we cannot change the mind of God, so why bother? Good question.

To that point, George Bernard Shaw was once quoted as saying, "Lots of people pray for me; and I have never been any worse for it. The only valid argument against the practice is the Glassite one that God knows his own business without prompting."

So why do we pray? There seems to be plenty of Scripture to support Mr. Shaw's sentiment. Jesus said to consider the lilies. They neither toil nor spin, yet even Solomon in all his glory was not arrayed like one of these

(Matt 6:28). If God can so clothe the grass that is alive one day and burned the next, why do we worry about clothing or food or drink? Your Father knows you have need of these things. Good point.

But regardless of the fact that God knows what you need and He knows the answer before the question, it is clear that praying is an integral and indispensable part of this relationship we have with God.

Consider Jesus. He prayed—a lot. And he had a lot to say about prayer. Don't think that you will be heard for your many pretty words. Enter privately into a closet and make your requests known. Never give up. Pray without ceasing.

I think to really understand what prayer is, we have to understand the prayer life of Jesus. To those who didn't know how to pray, He gave the Lord's Prayer which is very basic. His personal prayer life was on the other end of the spectrum, of a much higher degree. Have you ever wondered what he was praying for or about in the wilderness for forty days or high in those mountains all night by Himself? After all, He was the Son of God. Didn't He just carry on a conversation with God like we do with each other? What took so long?

First of all, though the Son of Man, He was also human and His communion with God was no different than yours or mine. He had to seek the will of God just like we do, the old fashioned way. But right there are the operative words; prayer is about finding God's will and bringing that into expression. It is not about making sure God knows our will and hoping and wishing He will bring it into being. Those prayers fall on deaf ears.

In the wilderness, Jesus firmed up the truth about Himself once and for all. He came away knowing His mission and the cup that was His to drink. After that, there was no going back. It was finished and He knew it. During His ministry, He often went into the mountains alone to center Himself in God's will. When He came down, He was filled up. There was nothing more to think about—just bring the Father's will into expression. There was no doubting, no questioning. He returned as the spontaneous expression of the Father. So much so that He could say,

[19] So Jesus said to them, "Truly, truly, I say to you, the Son can do nothing of his own accord, but only what he sees the Father doing. For whatever the Father does, that the Son does likewise. [20] For the Father loves the Son and shows him all that he himself is doing. And greater works than these will he show him, so that you may marvel."
(John 5:19-20)

And

"I can do nothing on my own. As I hear, I judge, and my judgment is just, because I seek not my own will but the will of him who sent me." (John 5:30)

Was He seeing visions or hearing voices as He ministered? No. He was saying that He and God were one Person. When He walked, God was walking. When He talked, God was talking. He understood union with the Father so much that He could say if you have seen me, you have seen the Father (John 14:9).

It is no different with us today. Once we understand the mystery which is Christ in us, once we understand that we live, yet not we, but Christ, it becomes clear. We are the will of God because we are one in union with Christ and Christ is one with God.

But he who is joined to the Lord becomes one spirit with him. (1Cor 6:17)

Once we become *knowers* of this truth, we realize that when we walk, Christ is walking. When we talk, Christ is talking. We take no thought. It is now easy to pray without ceasing, without effort. There is no begging. Prayer is nothing more than Christ in us urging us, pressing us, to speak His will into expression; to birth it so to speak. We don't change God's mind. We fulfill it.

XXV

COUNT IT ALL JOY – REALLY?

IN THE sixty fourth year and third month, on the fourth day of my birth I terminated the traditional role in the workplace. What most call retirement. I don't like that term. It sounds too much like being put out to pasture. I don't see myself as just grazing and chewing the cud from here on out.

Before the sun set on that day, before the sun rose on the golden era, my wife returned with the results of her medical tests. Cancer. Now stop the presses right here. I hadn't planned on vegging out on the beach or glutting on Netflix TV series, but I did think there might be a little of that, a little more ease. If I count picking potatoes in northern Maine, I've been working since I was ten years old. I admit, the picture I had of how this change of life would go was a little blurred, but I sure didn't see this coming. Golden years? Really?

Don't get me wrong. This isn't about me. I'm close and integral but still secondary to the situation. After all, I'm not the one with cancer. One thing I know, the timing of these two events was no coincidence. It was meant to be. The question we have to ask is why. What's in it for us ... or maybe others?

James says count it all joy when you meet trials. Many times I have spoken these same verses to mostly glazed over eyes. It just doesn't connect. Most of us have not really been in the fiery furnace. Sure, we have all had our trials. Maybe we lost a job, been ill, had financial problems, marital issues, personal problems, but when it comes down to life and death, face it ... the embers cool fast in comparison. When we do find others truly in the fiery furnace, it's at a distance. It's them, not us. We are sorry for them. We pray some nondescript prayers and then we move on with our lives. There is still a slight disconnect.

But then it isn't somebody else. It's you. Well-meaning Christians, probably like we did, come offering solace. "God is testing you," one might say. "You will be so much stronger when this is over," another soothes. Gee, we think. How lucky we are. Please don't let your envy be so obvious. Face it. You are alone. Or are you?

Now comes the time to walk that talk we have been preaching. Do we believe it all? Do we see God in every situation? I have to admit, I never saw anyone jump and click their heels when a real trial confronted them and I don't see us breaking the pattern. That probably confirms that the joy James refers to is something much more than a feeling. It's deeper. It doesn't dwell in the soul. Our soul feelings run the gamut, whipping us around in highs and lows. They are not all that trustworthy. It's in the spirit where truth, knowledge and will dwell.

Faith and prayer now become less abstract as we struggle to birth all that spirit knowledge into something that makes sense on an earthly level. What should we pray for? We pray for a complete cure. Is that selfish? That is our human desire of course. Even Jesus felt the anguish in His soul at Gethsemane. But that was all it was, human soul feelings temporarily reacting to appearances. But it wasn't God's will. Jesus said, "Don't judge by appearances but judge a righteous judgment." So He didn't.

I don't have all the answers. God knows how it works out because it was all finished in His mind before it started. Our prayer is to align ourselves with God's will, which is praising Him, knowing that it is finished and we eagerly await the manifestation of that finished work.

We have already seen the manifestations of God's work in others. The outpouring of love has flowed out of the bellies of Christian other lovers like rivers of living waters. This is for them as well as for us. The love has been overwhelming.

And we ... we are forced into total dependence on God. The steering and the brakes no longer respond. We no longer have control. Actually we never did. We knew that, but we had to be reminded. Our illusory dependence on ourselves, our abilities, our jobs, and our wealth reveals itself for what it is—clouds and wind with no rain. It has no power. It cannot save us. It's where moth and rust doth corrupt. That's all.

The real solace is this—this has not come upon us. It has come upon Christ. How, you ask? I thought this happened to me. Jesus said, "In that it has happened to one of these, it has happened to me." I'm putting a little twist on Matthew 25, but take my word for it, it's all the same. If it happens to us, it happens to Christ.

Do we believe the mystery which is Christ in us? Do we really believe, "I live, yet not I, but Christ (Gal 2:20)?" If you do, then you will see that God has brought this upon Himself for His glory. You may have thought it was meant for evil, but God meant it for good.

I would that God had placed this on me and not my wife. But that is Christ in me saying what He has already done. He has already taken it upon Himself. We may not know the exact outcome, but we know that if it has come upon Christ, we can praise God for His finished work. It is well with our soul.

XXVI

IS THERE A REST FOR THE PEOPLE OF GOD?

IS THERE a rest for the People of God? Today? In this time and place? One might wonder when you look around at the burdens some Christians seem to shoulder. In my book *The Lost Coin*, Sam Season walks down Church Street which has seven churches. The first one he hits is the Baptist Church:

The first was a Baptist church. They were already in the mode, sort of. He could hear "Just As I Am" faintly emanating from inside. Could use a little more enthusiasm, he thought. Sam had a soft spot for Baptists. You had to love them. Their heart seemed to be in the right place, but it was just too hard to get to heaven.

Doesn't that remind you of this old classic?

> *O land of rest, for thee I sigh!*
> *When will the moment come*
> *When I shall lay my armor by*
> *And dwell in peace at home?*
> *We'll work till Jesus comes,*
> *We'll work till Jesus comes,*

That song is not an unusual sentiment. Sure doesn't seem easy. I get tired just humming the lyrics. Or what about Alan Jackson singing his song *Where I Come From*?

> *I said where I come from it's cornbread and chicken*
> *Where I come from a lotta front porch sitin'*
> *Where I come from tryin' to make a livin'*
> ***And workin' hard to get to Heaven**, where I come from*

There are many people waiting for the next life to enjoy God. The question is what are they leaving on the table today? Jesus said,

> "[28] *Come to me, all who labor and are heavy laden, and I will give you rest.* [29] *Take my yoke upon you, and learn from me, for I am gentle and lowly in heart, and you will find rest for your souls.* [30] *For my yoke is easy, and my burden is light."* (Matt 11:28-30)

I like the sound of that a whole lot more. So let's answer the question once and for all and the answer is ... YES! Rest is available right here! Right now! How do we know?

Paul confirmed it in Hebrews:

> *"So then, there remains a Sabbath rest for the people of God, ..."* (Heb 4:9)

The key is how to obtain this rest because, I don't know about you, but I want it. After stating it available, he tells how in the next verse:

> *"for whoever has entered God's rest has also rested from his works as God did from his."* (Heb 4:10)

There you have it. Pretty easy, huh? We just need to rest from our own works. Well, easier said than done. This is the part that trips most of us up as we are constantly prodded to work *for* Jesus. We are created unto good works so we frantically start working for Jesus trying to force that fruit into existence. The problem is you can't work *for* Jesus, any more than Jesus could work *for* God. You can only let God work in you, through you, as you. Jesus was clear about that even He couldn't do the works.

> *"Truly, truly, I say to you, the Son can do nothing of his own accord, but only what he sees the Father doing. For whatever the Father does, that the Son does likewise."* (John 5:19)

The Father has already completed the works. The Son just brings them into manifestation. Jesus could say, "I live, yet not I, but the Father." Sound familiar? Yes ... it all circles back to:

> *"I am crucified with Christ: nevertheless I live; yet not I, but Christ liveth in me:"* (Gal 2:20)

If you believe this, then your work comes from a position of rest. The tree produces the fruit naturally, without any effort from the tree. It just manifests what it is. So do you.

XXVII

TO DENY OR NOT TO DENY

JESUS SAID to his disciples,

²⁴ "If anyone would come after me, let him deny himself and take up his cross and follow me. ²⁵ For whoever would save his life will lose it, but whoever loses his life for my sake will find it. ²⁶ For what will it profit a man if he gains the whole world and forfeits his soul? Or what shall a man give in return for his soul?" (Matt 16:24-26)

When you read these words—deny yourself and take up your cross—what images come to mind? Immediately I think of having to resist worldly temptations and shouldering a cross so heavy that even Jesus couldn't carry it to Golgotha on his own. It all sounds very hard and it seems to fly in the face of the ease Jesus promised.

²⁸ "Come to me, all who labor and are heavy laden, and I will give you rest. ²⁹ Take my yoke upon you, and learn *from me, for I am gentle and lowly in heart, and you will find rest for your souls. *^{30}* For my yoke is easy, and my burden is light."* (Matt 11:28-30)

So what is going on? I like the latter verses more than the former. Is this really about denying myself that second piece of cake or is it about something else? For sure, throughout history, many have taken this as the letter and denied themselves to the point of asceticism. They fear the natural pulls of the body. What is interesting is that there are no appetites of the body that are inherently evil. God provided us with them all for specific purposes. Of course, all can be abused and result in sin, but that is not what this is about. As always, Jesus is revealing something spiritual and deep.

First let's take a look at the background in Matthew 16. Jesus just had another altercation with the religious authorities of the day who continued to taunt and test him. He told the disciples to beware of the leaven of the Pharisees and Sadducees. They didn't get it so he had to explain he was referring to their teaching, not about the lack of bread.

The Pharisees and Sadducees had an affliction common to man even today.

*Then Jesus said to the crowds and to his disciples, *^{2}* "The scribes and the Pharisees sit on Moses' seat, *^{3}* so do and observe whatever they tell you, but not the works they do. For they preach, but do not practice ... *^{5}* They do all their deeds to be seen by others."* (Matt 23:1-3,5)

Why?

"for they loved the glory that comes from man more than the glory that comes from God." (John 12:43)

The bottom line is that the scribes and Pharisees made a choice. They said yes to self for self and said no to self for others. Whenever we say yes to one thing, that means we say no to another by default. They may have had the appearance of ministering to others, but in actuality they were in it for themselves.

The concept of denial is not about depriving ourselves. That is looking yet again through the wrong end of the telescope. It's about choosing one life over another. When we say yes to Jesus, who is the Life, we say no to the other life, the self for self life, which isn't life at all. Once we choose Jesus, we begin a new life that is so far superior to the old that it is ridiculous to try and make a comparison.

We no longer fear the world, its temptations, or our motives. We have the mind of Christ and we trust that our desires are His desires, if so be we are in the Spirit. And you are in the Spirit if Christ dwells in you. Then the burden is light and the yoke is easy because we live, yet not us, but Christ.

XXVIII

THE LONG ARM OF THE LAW

THE BIBLE is clear, we are saved by grace (Eph 2:8) and that by the works of the law no human being will be justified in his sight (Rom 3:20). The law, it says, only exists to bring our attention to the knowledge of sin. Once saved, we are no longer under the law (Rom 6:14). That sounds pretty good, huh? I'm free!!

It may seem clear enough, but this is probably one of the most difficult concepts for humans to apply. The law is everywhere. There is no escape. As I barrel down the highway twenty miles an hour over the speed limit, I know I risk being caught by the long arm of the law. When I tell him, "Sorry officer, I am not under the law," he will no doubt check me for drugs in addition to handing me my ticket.

It's clear there are consequences if we break the law of the land. There may be a few politicians or some of the rich and famous who are not under the law, but the rest of us are going to pay to the uttermost farthing.

In the context of Scripture, we are obviously talking about a different set of laws. So what are these laws and how does this work, us being exempt from them? Face it … many pastors and well-meaning fellow Christians quiver at the thought of total freedom. They think all hell will break loose if we don't keep some restrictions, some guardrails in place. So, what is the problem with a few regulations?

Let's be truthful. Few have actually freed themselves completely from the law. If you examine the language we use and the way we dance around grace and the law, it sure seems they are inextricably and surreptitiously mixed. Just as a little leaven leavens the whole lump, so has grace been leavened with the law. The law seems to engulf us in this haze we don't see. I remember one time driving to a chemical plant. As I crested the hill, I could see it was totally engulfed in a domelike chemical haze. When I arrived and brought it to their attention, they were totally clueless. They didn't see it. Their eyes had adjusted to the dimmer light.

There are a lot of buzzwords and innuendo that raise flags to this point. Someone mentions core values or a moral code, or we need to do this or we need to do that for Jesus because of what He did for us—no more than an obligation to pay Him back. We need to live for Jesus. All these things sound very righteous. Unfortunately, we have no righteousness other than Christ in us, and He doesn't need any competition.

The fact is grace and law can't be mixed any more than oil and water can mix. We are fooling ourselves if we believe they can. It's one or the other.

Adherence to any external law restricts our freedom in Christ and shows that we lack the faith to believe Christ in us is able to accomplish His purpose in us. Freedom from the law does not mean we have license to sin (Rom 6:1). And freedom from the law does not mean it is abolished—it means it is fulfilled. How?

"Do not think that I have come to abolish the Law or the Prophets; I have not come to abolish them but to fulfill them." (Matt 5:18)

Christ fulfilled it and if He fulfilled it, then it is already fulfilled in us because Christ dwells in our spirits. It becomes natural and spontaneous because the law is now who we are:

The Holy Spirit also testifies to us about this. First he says: [16] *"This is the covenant I will make with them after that time, says the Lord. I will put my laws in their hearts, and I will write them on their minds." (Heb 10:15-16)*

The thing—the *laws*—He put in us is Christ! And Christ is Love. The only thing hindering our freedom is unbelief. Christ is all we need.

For Christ is the end of the law for righteousness to everyone who believes. (Rom 10:4)

The only question remaining is do you believe?

XXIX

DO YOU HAVE A LOVE AFFAIR WITH THE LAW?

"WHAT? THAT'S an odd question to ask," you say. We all admit that the law is good, but, hey ... love it? Get serious. I don't know about you, but any interactions I had with the law were met with more trepidation than any warm embrace of love. Yet, at least one person of God seems to take a different perspective. David says,

Oh how I love your law!
It is my meditation all the day. (Ps 119:97)

It seems a little dry to sit and meditate on the Ten Commandments for any length of time. Yet there was something about the Law that David took such pleasure in he couldn't think of anything else. For someone who was a pretty egregious law breaker himself, you might have thought he had more to fear than delight in. What was it that so excited him? What was it that he had learned that swallowed up all fear and anxiety of the law to the point of loving it?

For sure, it was more than meditating on the written words of the Law. He knew that the Ten Commandments were much more than an external code of conduct to live by. There was a deeper meaning underlying these words, something that God was trying to tell us about Himself. Throughout the Bible, God communicates to us things that are spiritual, things that are in heaven, the only way He can—in simple earthly terms.

The Ten Commandments are no exception. David knew that the written law was spiritual, that it was telling us the essence of who God is and that it is the exact representation of His nature. In the simplest words possible, GOD IS THE LAW!

To really understand what that means, we need to develop this a little further:

If God IS The Law

And we know that:

God IS Love

Then we can also say:

The Law IS Love

If these are hard sayings, it is only because of the outside in perspective we have the Law. We see the Law as outside of us, engraved on stone, something cold and hard and unforgiving. Though we know that love fulfills the law (Rom 13:10), we may not get the connection how the law fulfills love because it is love.

That may sound good in some nebulous way, but what does it all mean? Why do I need to know this and what is wrong with the written code? There is nothing wrong with the written code, but it served its purpose. It was only meant to be temporary, our schoolmaster (Gal. 3:24) until it was replaced with something better. Its purpose was to show us who He is, who we are, and the insurmountable chasm between us. If we were like God, then we would take to the commandments like a duck takes to water. It would be natural. But in our lost condition, in the weakness of our flesh, it isn't. The law is there for the lawless, revealing our inability to keep it. We needed something better and God did that by sending His Son to us.

³ For God has done what the law, weakened by the flesh, could not do. By sending his own Son in the likeness of sinful flesh and for sin, he condemned sin in the flesh, ⁴ in order that the righteous requirement of the law might be fulfilled in us, who walk not according to the flesh but according to the Spirit. (Rom 8:3-4)

Now that we have Christ, we are no longer under the law (Rom 6:14). It is passé. Yet, somehow without it, the scripture says we can fulfill the righteous requirement of the law. But we have to walk according to the Spirit, not the flesh. How does that work? God tells us through Jeremiah:

For this is the covenant that I will make with the house of Israel after those days, declares the Lord: I will put my law within them, and I will write it on their hearts. And I will be their God, and they shall be my people. (Jer 31:33)

Now we are getting close. God says I will put my Law *IN* you. It becomes part of you—internalized. It is now who you are, not something you *try* to be. It happens in your spirit. Paul explains this in Christ:

To them God chose to make known how great among the Gentiles are the riches of the glory of this mystery, which is Christ in you, the hope of glory. (Col 1:27)

Jeremiah and this verse are one and the same. Christ is God. God is Love. God is the Law. The Law is Love. And now all that indwells you. Your spirit joins in union with Christ and they are one spirit:

But he who is joined to the Lord becomes one spirit with him. (1Cor 6:17)

If you are one with Christ, then you are one with the Law, one with Love. This is the Gospel—the Good News. We love the Law because we love God. We no longer have to pretend to keep the law—we *are* the Law.

If that is such good news, why do so many Christians hang on to the external law with its dos and don'ts knowing it never worked then and it doesn't work now? It is because they still consider it from distance, not realizing how close it is. Whereas it should be the love of their life, it only brings condemnation. As long as you focus on the external law, you will be forever under its spell and can be assured that you will cast yourself in prison and not come out until you have paid the last penny (Matt5:25-26).

Instead of *trying* to fulfill the Law, *be* the Law! Know that the Law indwells you, that Christ lives in you, through you, as you.

I am crucified with Christ: nevertheless I live; yet not I, but Christ liveth in me: and the life which I now live in the flesh I live by the faith of the Son of God, who loved me, and gave himself for me. (Gal 2:20)

Christ is the only one that can fulfill the Law. But that is only if you *let* Him, the hardest three letter word in the English language. The only thing that hinders is unbelief. Therefore believe!

XXX

LOVE IS GOD

OFTEN IN our reading of scripture, we can miss some unique revelations God desires for us to have. It is easy to miss deep meanings from very familiar verses, verses we know by heart, verses we have read over and over. Lectio divina, or sacred reading, is an ancient way of listening to scripture. The text is read slowly and prayerfully allowing the Holy Spirit, who is always at work hovering over the face of the deep, to manifest the unseen into existence.

Let's start with one verse everyone knows, believers and non-believers alike:

God is love (1 John 4:8).

Let's mull that one over and see what God is really saying about himself. God is love. God is love. Now, if all you are hearing is what is on the surface, that love is a characteristic of God, then you are probably missing the real message.

Let's use a little algebra to make the point. "Oh, no!" you say as nightmares of the infamous unknown x reemerge to haunt you. But calm down; this will be a very easy lesson. Let's start with our first reading:

God is love (1 John 4:8)

Remember the symmetric axiom? It says that if X=Y, then conversely Y=X. So, let's flip it around. This is what you get:

Love is God!

Now what do you see? Hear? Has the meaning changed? Has it unearthed something that heretofore was hidden from us? Let's add some emphasis:

*Love **IS** God!*

Not to revisit one president's trademark retort, "it depends on what the meaning of is is," but that is what we are talking about in this context.

You might think this is a play on words, but it is not. You see, love is not something that God has. It is not an attribute or a quality. It is *WHO HE IS*. Love is a Person and that Person is God. God is Spirit. This is the essence of God—WHO HE IS.

Likewise, we can take similar scriptures, God is wisdom, God is light, etc. and use the same law to better describe the essence of God:

Wisdom is God (1 Cor 1:30)

Light is God (1 John 1:5)

All those things we think we have such as love and wisdom are nothing more than earthly shadows of True Love that exist solely as the Person God, the true agape love that lays its life down for another without thought or hesitation.

And now for the beautiful part, the Good News—all those things that God is, His Essence, dwell in us in Christ. How? Because we are one spirit with him:

But he who is joined to the Lord becomes one spirit with him. (1Cor 6:17)

God manifests Love—Himself—through us in Christ. It is not the kind of love based on soul feelings that change like the wind. This Love is spirit and truth and never varies.

So, if you thought it was impossible to love the unlovable things or persons in your life, now you know it is possible. It has nothing to do with a feeling. It is no longer us living and loving, but Christ living and loving in us, as us, without respect of persons. Amen to that.

XXXI

NATURAL DISASTERS — AN ACT OF GOD?

AS HURRICANE Matthew barreled toward South Florida, I thought this was it. With a mixture of nervousness and anticipation, we were ready for our first hurricane. We stocked our provisions and battened down the hatches waiting for the worst and the inevitable power outage. But the lights didn't even flicker. To our relief, it skirted just far enough east of us that it was a non-event. It didn't even rattle the shutters.

That, of course, was not the case for many. It mowed down Haiti and wrecked half of the eastern seaboard. Social media, the platform for all wannabe savants regardless of qualification, couldn't help but debate the attribution of this hit or miss destruction to God versus dumb luck. Someone started it with how "we were so lucky that the hurricane went around us and we were spared." That person was immediately corrected by one of the faithful writing, "No, we weren't lucky. We have the mercy of Jesus Christ to thank for sparing us."

That, of course, set up a schoolyard brawl as facebookers ducked their heads, closed their eyes and flailed their digital arms at each other. "Oh yeah," one responds, "Jesus spared you while he killed hundreds of Haitians and destroyed everyone else's lives. If that is your god, you can have him."

So which is it? Is it God or luck of the draw when good and evil descend with no respect of persons? If we believe it is arbitrary luck, fine; we drop it right there. But if it is God, then we have a big problem coming to terms that one God could deal out both without distinction between the two. Most Christians deal with it by ascribing "good" things to God while saying He "allows" evil. That is a way of letting Him off the hook. No, you can't have it both ways. If one is true, so must be the other. If it is true that it was God who showed "mercy" on one group, then it must be equally true that it was God who showed "wrath" on the other. Since it is a fact that God is good (1 Tim 4:4) and that God is love (1 John 4:8), then in either case, whether you call it wrath or whether you call it mercy, God must be displaying love in some form because He cannot operate from anything other than who He is.

The reason even believers have difficulty with this seeming contradistinction is the notion that things are divided into two groups—good and evil. Good is when we get what we want. God is blessing us. Evil is the opposite—when we don't get what we want. How many times have you heard someone say how blessed they were when they got the job they wanted or they got that monetary windfall. Others jealously wonder why they have not been so blessed. The leaven of the so-called prosperity gospel has created a sense of entitlement equating God's blessing with material wealth and status. They want the best of two worlds and Jesus said you can't have both (Matt 6:24). They have left their first love in pursuit of worldly blessings.

But, God doesn't see it that way. Jesus said in Matthew and Luke that if your eye is healthy, your whole body will be full of light.

The light of the body is the eye: if therefore thine eye be single, thy whole body shall be full of light. (Matt 6:22 KJV)

Jesus is saying there is only one power in the universe, not two. That means there is nothing done under heaven that doesn't have God's signature on it and, if so, then everything He does is for your good even if it doesn't "feel" so good. God says He makes peace and He creates evil (Isa 45:7), both for a single purpose—Love. Anything that comes between us and God will be taken away.

Disasters like this reveal either our divided outlook or our ability to see with the Single Eye. If you find yourself cursing God, then all you lost was a house built on sand that was destined to be washed away (Matt 7:26-27). This may sound callous and sanctimonious, but even loss of life reveals the same thing. If you loved your life more on this earth than God, then you traded eternal life for a bowl of stew.

Whoever loves his life loses it, and whoever hates his life in this world will keep it for eternal life. (John 12:25)

The truth is we are so concerned with the first death, which is inevitable, that we give little thought to the second death (Rev 20:14) which has the power to separate us from God forever. Paul says that whether in life or death, Christ will be honored in his body (Phil 1:20) and he also said something that is totally contrary to this love affair we have with the world.

For to me to live is Christ, and to die is gain. (Phil 1:21)

Sounds like he knew something many of us are missing.

Regarding material prosperity, loss of or lack thereof, Paul said it was also of no matter. Whether a have or a have-not, we are to be content as Paul learned:

[11] Not that I am speaking of being in need, for I have learned in whatever situation I am to be content. [12] I know how to be brought low, and I know how to abound. In any and every circumstance, I have learned the secret of facing plenty and hunger, abundance and need. (Phil 4:11-12)

These truths cut to the chase of who we are in Christ. John divides believers into children, young men, and fathers (1 John 2:12-14). Knowing that God uses all things for our good (Rom 8:28) whether we call it good or evil separates the mature from the immature in Christ. Knowing who you are in Christ is a sign of fatherhood in the gospel. True Life is knowing we have already died in Christ and it is no longer we who live, but Christ lives in us (Gal 2:20). Then we understand what it means "to live *is* Christ" and all is Good.

XXXII

WHO TO VOTE FOR—WHAT WOULD JESUS DO?

IT'S WITH a little trepidation I step into this topic. I am not a social activist. Though some have claimed that Jesus was a social activist, he most certainly was not. The only thing he said about Rome was "render to Caesar the things that are Caesar's, and to God the things that are God's (Matt 22:21)." The Jews, however, thought he was. Though they may have despised Rome's rule, they were quite comfortable with the status quo and were afraid Jesus would upset the limited power they enjoyed.

> *"If we let him go on like this, everyone will believe in him, and the Romans will come and take away both our place and our nation."* (John 11:48)

Though Jesus' coming was going to have radical consequences to the entire world, He was clear that His kingdom had nothing to do with the current systems of government. They were not his concern. He said to Pontius Pilate:

Jesus answered, "My kingdom is not of this world. If my kingdom were of this world, my servants would have been fighting, that I might not be delivered over to the Jews. But my kingdom is not from the world." (John 18:36)

This concept was beyond the understanding of the Jews and the world even today and even among many Christians. If he had been interested in altering the status quo, he would have fought. But His kingdom was beyond the touch of earthly regimes and had already been established. He had no vocal criticism of Rome's rule. The only criticism he had was against the ecclesiastical hierarchy of the day, the only government he was concerned with.

Now that doesn't give us much of a clue as we face an election of poor choices which may have radical consequences for our earthly nation. Though we may not be of this world (John 17:16), we are still in it. We have feet planted in both worlds and we are accountable for what we do here on earth.

So what do you do? I have this simplistic belief that all peoples get the government they deserve, particularly democratic societies. And that is what we have whether you like it or not—we get what we deserve. We can cry and whine about a government that has been self-serving, favors one class of people over another, says one thing and does another that mysteriously profits them while the poor man ends up paying the band, but we asked for it.

At one time, I had this naïve notion that we needed to eliminate everyone in Congress and start over. I would vote against every incumbent. I thought this generation needed to die out like the Israelites in the wilderness before they could possess the Promised Land. I failed. No one lined up behind me. We continued to send the same ones back to Washington over and over and over. But it wouldn't have worked. Even if they all started with good intentions, they would quickly learn the means of survival as our "servants" and that generally means becoming tainted by the system.

And now the chickens have come home to roost. Our choices are a narcissistic, greedy, pathological lying wrecking ball with no coherent ideology and a narcissistic, greedy pathological lying liberal who thinks "we need to change religious beliefs." I didn't know that was any human's job.

Religious leaders have weighed in on the election purporting to be oracles of the will of God for you. Evangelicals seem to back Trump more, i.e. the Republican Party, giving the false impression that conservatism and/or church attendance are commensurate with Christianity. They are not. They, of all people, should know that the only solution to the world's ill is Jesus Christ. But because the prospect of that solution is so bleak, they have fallen back to Plan B, supporting those who will legislate their version of morality. There is a reason Jesus didn't join the fray of politics. He fought a different front in a different dimension, the one that was from *another world*, the one that changes the hearts of people through the gospel.

Clinton represents the establishment, the same ol' same ol' liberal agenda which strikes fear into their hearts. There is plenty of nefarious smoke rising out of both pits, but be careful to fault them. They are simply a product of the system we helped create. She learned better than most how the system works, how one hand washes the other and then how to cover it up. Her opponent says he has washed their (the establishment) hands, admittedly for his personal gain, but never had his hands washed and claims that as a virtue.

Now, if one of your criteria is to have a Christian leader, you should carefully consider both candidates.

You might be disappointed. Jesus said, "Judge not, that you be not judged (Matt 7:1)," so we have to be careful. But at the same time Paul didn't let us off the hook when it came to an obligation to judge when the need stares us in the face.

Do you not know that we are to judge angels? How much more, then, matters pertaining to this life! (1Cor 6:3)

So you be the judge. Because someone says they are a Christian doesn't make it so. Because they attend church doesn't make it so. Being a conservative or a liberal has nothing to do with it. We don't look at what they say or what party they belong to. We look at what they do and we have plenty of material to assess for both candidates. As much as I hate clichés, if it walks like a duck and it quacks like a duck and it looks like a duck, then it's a duck regardless of how someone spins it.

So, now for the famous question—what would Jesus do? Well, the answer is in what He did. When things started getting heavy, he would climb up a mountain by himself to pray. He would enter his closet and close the door to all the noise of the outside world and earthly senses. When He came back down, he was so totally aligned with the will of God that He could say,

"I can do nothing on my own. As I hear, I judge, and my judgment is just, because I seek not my own will but the will of him who sent me." (John 5:30)

It is the same with you. You don't need someone to tell you what the will of God is for you. If you understand the mystery, which is Christ in you (Col 1:27), then you do the same thing. You crawl into your closet, shut the door of the senses, the spin meisters, your friends, your pastors, and come out so aligned with God's will that you also can say the same thing Jesus said,

> ... *"Truly, truly, I say to you, the Son can do nothing of his own accord, but only what he sees the Father doing. For whatever the Father does, that the Son does likewise.*
> *(John 5:19)*

If you understand your union with Christ, how you are one with Him, then when you come out and enter the voting booth, it will be you voting, yet not you, but Christ who lives in you (Gal 2:20).

You can't go wrong. If you don't know your union with Christ, then you will be driven by the waves of someone else's self-serving rhetoric aimed to manipulate you for their personal gain. This, by the way, is how we got here in the first place. But regardless, the outcome will be what we deserve.

XXXIII

HAVE YOU LOST YOUR FIRST LOVE?

HAVE YOU lost your first love? Most Christians are probably oblivious to what that even means. It is not something we are necessarily cognizant of yet it is no small thing. That was made clear In Revelation when the Son of Man called the church of Ephesus to task on this very real condition.

> "² *I know your works, your toil and your patient endurance, and how you cannot bear with those who are evil, but have tested those who call themselves apostles and are not, and found them to be false.* ³ *I know you are enduring patiently and bearing up for my name's sake, and you have not grown weary.* ⁴ *But I have this against you, that you have abandoned the love you had at first."*
> (Rev 2:2-4)

Now that is quite a reprimand! I mean my goodness. He tells them that he knows their toil and patience, that they endure patiently for his name, that their relentless toil is second to none. And that is not good enough? Seriously? Can you work too earnestly for Him?

It seems harsh. They have worked diligently for the kingdom of God and now find themselves being rebuked ... lacking. But lacking what? What is this love they had at first that they have been accused of abandoning? Is it this?

And he answered, "You shall love the Lord your God with all your heart and with all your soul and with all your strength and with all your mind, and your neighbor as yourself." (Luke 10:27)

Have we abandoned our love for God? But don't the works prove our love, our faith? Remember what James said—faith without works is dead. So didn't Ephesus prove their faith, their love, by their tireless toil?

Well, the answer is yes and no. It's a slippery slope. Faith and works are two inseparable sides of the same coin. One is the fruit of the other. Works are the spontaneous outgrowth of faith. But works by themselves are not the job. Works without faith, without love, are also dead. Jesus made it clear that that is another real possibility.

[22] On that day many will say to me, 'Lord, Lord, did we not prophesy in your name, and cast out demons in your name, and do many mighty works in your name?' [23] And then will I declare to them, 'I never knew you; depart from me, you workers of lawlessness.' (Matt 7:22-23)

I wouldn't put Ephesus in that category, but it is clear that something has happened that has shifted their priorities. If you remember, when we began as Christians, we simply joyed being in and loving Christ and being loved by Christ. Our burdens were lifted. It was easy, spontaneous. Works were the effortless fruit born on branches just abiding in the vine. But later, things can change. In our zeal for Christ the branches can start to take on a life of their own and we forget who we are and what produces the fruit—the vine.

I am the vine; you are the branches. Whoever abides in me and I in him, he it is that bears much fruit, for apart from me you can do nothing. (John 15:5)

We look around us, judge by appearances, and see all the great works others are doing and wonder why our fruit is not up to par. We start to shoulder the load ourselves even though Jesus was clear that He did the lifting. We start to work *for* Christ which is the epitome of ridiculousness. You can't work *for* Christ as if you were paying Him back for all He has done for you. That would be wages due and defeat grace. It doesn't work like that.

It is easy to fall prey to a work ethic that quenches the Spirit. As soon as we are born again, we are inundated with a plethora of advice, books, tapes, sermons, constant exhortations, all of which tell us how to become a better Christian and what we should be doing as a child of God. We get twenty one ways on how to become a better Christian, ten ways on how to improve our prayer life, five ways on how to witness, and so on. Often, Christ is hardly mentioned at all or maybe tagged on the end. But the truth is they are more self-help, more self-improvement than promoting a deeper relationship with our true love—Christ.

An image is created of a fantasy Christian full of power and the Spirit. Everyone except us lives in an

Ozzie and Harriet world. Immediately we compare ourselves to this fictional character. We compare ourselves to what others who appear to be blessed are doing, and guess what? We find ourselves lacking. Big time. We don't pray enough. We don't read our Bible enough. We don't witness enough. We rob God of His tithe. We don't do our fair share in the church. The list goes on.

Just because it doesn't reflect reality doesn't stop us from shooting for the moon. Rather than *let* Christ be formed in us (Gal 4:19), we set out to make it happen ourselves, to prove our love. Whether we admit it or not, we have now become more concerned about conforming to the will of others than to the will of Christ.

Before long, keeping up appearances becomes more important than resting in Christ and just letting Him do his work through us, as us. We forget who we are. We forget our first love. We don't wait on the Lord. *We'll work till Jesus comes.* Ready or not.

So, let's get it back. Let's return to our first love. Remember how easy it was back then? We just basked in the grace of the Lord. Get back to the basics. Let Him do the works. Present your bodies a living sacrifice (Rom 12:1). That is your true spiritual worship. Imitate Christ by doing what He did which was just *letting* the Father do the works. Get your foot off the accelerator. He will do the driving. That is how Jesus did it.

> *So Jesus said to them, "Truly, truly, I say to you, the Son can do nothing of his own accord, but only what he sees the Father doing. For whatever the Father does, that the Son does likewise.* (John 5:19)

Remember who you are in Christ. Just as the Father lived in Christ and did the works, even so does Christ live in you and He does the works. We are simply branches abiding in the vine, vessels containing Him. *Let* Him live, not you. It's that easy.

> *I am crucified with Christ: nevertheless I live; yet not I, but Christ liveth in me: and the life which I now live in the flesh I live by the faith of the Son of God, who loved me, and gave himself for me.* (Gal 2:20)

XXXIV

ATHEISM VS THEISM

DO YOU know any atheists? It seems like they are becoming louder on the world stage, so I thought it would be interesting to examine their beliefs a little bit, but so far I have only found out what they profess not to believe. Even the definition is kind of squirmy. Webster says an atheist is *a person who believes God does not exist.* Another definition is *a person who disbelieves or lacks belief in the existence of God or gods.* I'm not sure what the difference is between one who disbelieves and one who lacks belief. I'll have to leave that to greater brains than mine.

I did find that not all atheists are *purists*. Some do believe in some sort of Supreme Being. Some believe in something called Intelligent Design, which I think is some kind of back handed compliment to the maybe Supreme Being. Like vegetarians that may eat a little chicken, they also tend to wander outside strict dogma obscuring their identity.

They have become more vocal, even mounting a battle against narrow minded believers and the shackles of religion. I would call them more antitheists then atheists. I'm not sure why they care because I don't think they do. They don't like others ramming religion down their throats and I can understand that.

But I'm not here to pick on atheists. What I want to point out is that they are not that special. There isn't as much difference as you think between their beliefs and many that profess to believe in God, god, or gods.

Being a simple man, I am going to try and boil this down to the essentials. *A-theist* means not theist. Therefore, the entire world is made up of two subsets—the ones that are not and the ones that are, the a-theists and the theists.

Let's start with the theists. They all think they are right; they are the ones going to heaven; everyone else is going to hell (or at least not going to participate in the invitation only private club of paradise). But believing in God or gods is no ticket to anywhere. James popped that balloon. Of course, if you are not a Christian, you don't care what James said, but it certainly is worth pondering.

> *You believe that God is one; you do well. Even the demons believe—and shudder!* (James 2:19)

Then there are the a-theists, the not theists. They know there ain't no heaven and they pray there ain't no hell. When you die, you die. End of story. They believe in human nature, themselves, love, aliens, reincarnation, whatever. Since they have no standard belief or creed, they are all over the map. The atheists will claim the others, the theists, are simply brainwashed dummies echoing beliefs that they don't even understand. And one could argue that to be the case with many, including Christians. They are what they are because of the environment they experienced.

Without getting into the weeds of any specific beliefs, I want to introduce a simple concept called *Truth*. I'm sure you have all heard of it. This is what all these groups claim to have a lock on. There is just one problem—there is only One Truth! I know that contemporary thinking says there are many paths to god or God or something or someone, except for that to be true they all have to converge on the same Final Destination because there can be only one Truth. Now this is scary because I am pretty sure we are not all heading in the same direction.

THE ONE THING THEISTS AND ATHEISTS AGREE ON

I hate to say it, but somebody has to be wrong. I am not going to say who, but one thing is for sure, whenever we say yes to one thing, we say no to the other. If we say yes to the Truth, we say no to the lie. Common sense dictates that those who say no to the Truth must be saying yes to something else—the untruth. So, what in the world are they saying yes to?

Ahhh ... the greatest question of all time—what is Truth? Well, whatever it is, we can say that Truth needs no Champion! It has no need to defend itself. It just is. The wind can blow this way and that, but it just stands there ... immutable. Those that feel they must justify their version of the truth are de facto saying they are not quite sure. They want validation.

For example, a well-known comedian loves to integrate his hatred for religion in his routine for laughter and applause, but all he is doing is seeking validation of his beliefs and is nothing more than a puppet operated by his audience. He has no clue.

You have to ask yourself the question—just what do you really believe? If you have chosen something other than Truth, if you are unsure, then let me be crystal clear—your belief is nothing more than a figment of your imagination. It is totally fabricated. You made it up or someone else made it up and put in your head. It doesn't exist anywhere other than in your mind. You may laugh at the Fairy Tales, the Easter Bunny or Santa Claus, but you just placed yourself in similar company.

It might be time for some serious introspection. You cannot not believe in something. If the earth you walk on and air you breathe is not enough evidence to start you with the idea of God, then what does trigger your beliefs? If you think when you die you just sail off into the sunset, then you better be sure of what is on the other side.

I know in what I have believed. I have no need to convince anyone. Truth needs no Champion! Can you say the same thing?

XXXV

THE SINGLE EYE

HAVE YOU ever heard someone say, "I have a praise," and then they go on to tell you how greatly the Lord has blessed them because they just got something they wanted or some situation worked out in their favor. "God is so good!" they say.

Here is an example. My friend says to me, "God is so good. Our house sold in a week! Full price nonetheless! God has truly blessed us!"

Now, isn't that nice, I think with a tinge of jealousy. *They must be so righteous because God is blessing them.* On the other hand, I must not be so righteous because I'm not quite so blessed. I have a house to sell that is worth one hundred thousand less than I paid for it because of the subprime debacle and it's been sitting there a year and a half with no offer. What am I supposed to say then ... when I not only don't get what I want, it keeps getting worse? Do I say, "God is so bad?" Or maybe I say grudgingly, "God is good," but He is disciplining me because He does that to the ones He loves (Heb 12:6). Maybe they should be the jealous one, eh?

This example is actually quite trivial in the grand scheme of things, but it's typical of the situations we are confronted with daily. Most just create unnecessary anxieties that slink into embarrassment when we or others are confronted with really serious life and death situations over which we have no control. We pray for someone to be healed because it's the righteous thing to do, but we know that God doesn't always heal. The opposite happens. People die. We don't feel like praising God. Saying, "God is good," sounds tinny, hollow, insincere. We ask, "Why ... why do bad things happen to good people? Where is God in this?"

Whether we approve the outcome or not, we have to preserve the belief in the truth—that God is good in all our circumstances and He really does work all things for our good, to those who have been called according to His purpose (Rom 8:28). Otherwise, our faith is lie. God is always good. God doesn't change. That is His eternal nature. He can't work contrary to his fixed nature which is Love.

The problem is we tend to look at things through the natural mind of man and not the mind of God. Remember the altercation between Jesus and Peter when Jesus divulged to His disciples His purpose, that He would be taken and killed and rise the third day? Peter jumps up and rebukes him.

And Peter took him aside and began to rebuke him, saying, "Far be it from you, Lord. This shall never happen to you." (Matt 16:22)

That sounds mighty righteous, doesn't it? That might even be something we would say. How could we let this *evil* happen to our Lord? So, how did Jesus respond?

But he turned and said to Peter, "Get behind me, Satan! You are a hindrance to me. For you are not setting your mind on the things of God, but on the things of man."
(Matt 16:23)

Wow! Talk about a rebuke from the Lord! What did he do wrong? Well, he reverted into his *natural man* mode and judged by appearances. Remember what Jesus said about appearances? They can be hazardous to your health.

"Do not judge by appearances, but judge with right judgment." (John 7:24)

The only way to judge with right judgment is to be spiritually discerning. Hmmmm ... easier said than done? Well, it is within our grasp. After all, we do have the mind of Christ (1 Cor 2:16). The question might be how to exercise this gift? Jesus gave us many clues, but this is my favorite.

"The eye is the lamp of the body. So, if your eye is healthy (single, simple, whole), your whole body will be full of light, [23] but if your eye is bad, your whole body will be full of darkness. If then the light in you is darkness, how great is the darkness!" (Matt 6:22-23)

The word translated healthy in the ESV means single or simple. I like simple. It means there is only one power in the universe! Not two. To say on one hand that God is good when it appears to benefit us but be sullen on the other hand when it doesn't is because of a duplicitous outlook. To have a *Single Eye* means we see God in everything, in every circumstance in our lives whether we perceive it to be *good* or *evil*. If you have a dual outlook, a belief in two powers, your whole body will be full of darkness.

The wonderful thing about this is that it destroys all the fear and alleged power of evil. The only power it ever had was the power you allowed it. It also removes the burden of judging by appearances. God will always turn the appearance of evil to our good. Given that truth, you can now relax and let God do the work. If you don't believe me, ask Joseph.

As for you, you meant evil against me, but God meant it for good, ... (Gen 50:20)

XXXVI

WHAT DOES CHRIST LOOK LIKE?

A LONG time ago, there was a painter. He painted a large portrait of Christ. Of course, no one really knows what Jesus looked like. That is by design, because if we had his image, no doubt some would worship the image and not the Christ. But this one was different. Granted, it probably bore no resemblance to the man, but it was the perfect representation and picture of the Christ.

So, what do you mean, you might ask? How was this portrait different? Well, if you got up really close to it, and you might need a magnifying glass, you would see that the painting was created out of tiny individual letters. Yes, it was actually the written Word of God with inflections and various sizes and shades so that when you stood back, behold! There was the image of Christ! In today's digital jargon, we would say the letters were the pixels used to create the image.

How apropos. For the entire Bible is a portrait of God. It's not just a bunch of words on a page. It's not just a bunch of history as some would say. It is the Word, the expression of God! Just like Christ, the Word of God made flesh, was the perfect expression and representation of the Father.

The Bible is full of images, metaphors, and allegories to communicate heavenly things in earthly terms. I want to present another portrait of Christ using Paul's metaphor of the body of Christ. He said,

[12]"For just as the body is one and has many members, and all the members of the body, though many, are one body, so it is with Christ. [13] For in one Spirit we were all baptized into one body—Jews or Greeks, slaves or free—and all were made to drink of one Spirit." (1Cor 12:12-13)

Paul is saying that WE ARE the body of Christ, comprised of many members, both metaphorically and in actuality. We know that our own bodies are the temple of God (1 Cor3:16) and that Christ lives in us (Gal 2:20). We therefore manifest Christ both individually and corporately. He in us, as us.

You might think these words are a bit risky, putting ourselves on an equal basis with Christ. Am I saying we are God? Of course not. Just like a drop of water is not the ocean, the ocean manifests itself in the form of many drops. We are simply vessels that contain Christ. We are the vehicle through which He manifests Himself on earth. Remember that God is Spirit and has no form. He must manifest himself through his creation. In case it hasn't dawned on you yet, we're it! Jesus said if you have seen me, you have seen the Father. Likewise, when you have seen us, you have seen Christ.

Now, let's go back to the painting. Substitute the letters with the myriad of Christians that make up the body of Christ. They are of all sizes, shapes, and colors. Now stand back. What do you see? Christ!

There is still one more lesson to learn from this metaphor. We are not all the same! Paul elaborates:

> [14] *For the body does not consist of one member but of many.* [15] *If the foot should say, "Because I am not a hand, I do not belong to the body," that would not make it any less a part of the body.* [16] *And if the ear should say, "Because I am not an eye, I do not belong to the body," that would not make it any less a part of the body.* [17] *If the whole body were an eye, where would be the sense of hearing? If the whole body were an ear, where would be the sense of smell?* [18] *But as it is, God arranged the members in the body, each one of them, as he chose.* [19] *If all were a single member, where would the body be?* [20] *As it is, there are many parts, yet one body.* (1Cor 12:14-20)

This is important because too often we conform to the corporate voice rather than God's as to what our gifts and calling are. For example, some churches may think that everyone should be an evangelist. True, we all are by default to one degree or another, but some are specifically called to this mission and some are not. If all were evangelists, we would be left with a few million babies out there with stunted growth. That might be like running on two left legs or just one leg. If all were teachers, there might not be many to teach.

No, we all have our own calling. They are all different. Some are teachers, some are prophets, some are leaders, and some just have the gift of love or faith, my favorites. Some are prominent and some are obscure, but all necessary. If others try to engage you in their personal cause, approach it prayerfully. It may also be your calling or it may not.

XXXVII

WHAT DOES SATAN LOOK LIKE?

WRITING ABOUT Satan is a bit risky. Most people figure he is out there somewhere but really don't think of him as an up close and personal presence in their lives. They prefer to keep him under the bed.

First of all, do you even believe in a person called Satan? If you do, then you have to wonder where he is, what he looks like, and what he is up to. If you don't, his work is done and he is happy. One thing about Satan, he is ingenious at cloaking his existence. He is not called the Deceiver for nothing. And he has several effective tricks.

First he promotes himself as a red cartoon character with horns, tail, and pitchfork. Pretty clever, huh? That works for the simple minded; it's good for a laugh. But he is much deadlier and clever than that. He can handle the intellectual of intellectuals with ease. Let's see how he did it in the beginning, in the Garden; his first contact with humans. Eve tells Satan,

> *"but God said, 'You shall not eat of the fruit of the tree that is in the midst of the garden, neither shall you touch it, lest you die." (Gen 3:3)*

Satan replies:

> *[4] But the serpent said to the woman, "You will not surely die. [5] For God knows that when you eat of it your eyes will be opened, and you will be like God, knowing good and evil." (Gen 3:4-5)*

Satan tricks Eve by obfuscating the truth. He mixes some truth in with the lie. You might call him the Great Obfuscator. No, she didn't die. Not physically ... not yet anyway. But she died to God instantaneously. Did they become like God knowing good and evil? In a sense. Now they shared the delusion of independence promulgated by Satan and now falsely believed they were lords of their own destiny. How wrong!

At that point, Satan became the ruler of this world (John 14:30). Right there, most people are going to pause. Sure, we have evil in this world, he certainly has influence, but ruler? Really? He doesn't rule me.

Really? Let's see. What did Jesus say?

> *[42] Jesus said to them, "If God were your Father, you would love me, for I came from God and I am here. I came not of my own accord, but he sent me. [43] Why do*

you not understand what I say? It is because you cannot bear to hear my word. ⁴⁴ You are of your father the devil, and your will is to do your father's desires. He was a murderer from the beginning, and does not stand in the truth, because there is no truth in him. When he lies, he speaks out of his own character, for he is a liar and the father of lies. (John 8:42-44)

Mighty strong language, huh? What is more interesting is he was speaking to the religious leaders.

Even Christians have a hard time swallowing this one. Surely he wasn't speaking of me? I was bad, sure, but not that bad. Well, before you received Jesus Christ as your Lord and Savior, the answer was yes. He was speaking of all of us. We were all born the same way. Maybe we had no strong consciousness of it, but it was so. I didn't say it. Jesus said it and Paul confirmed it.

² in which you once walked, following the course of this world, following the prince of the power of the air, the spirit that is now at work in the sons of disobedience—³ among whom we all once lived in the passions of our flesh, carrying out the desires of the body and the mind, and were by nature children of wrath, like the rest of mankind. (Eph 2:2-3)

This again dispels the two nature myth as well as the myth that we were ever independent or had a nature of our own. We take on the nature of our Father. Before it was the devil, now it is Christ, if so be you are in Christ.

Now you are looking at me like I have two heads. Sorry, it's the truth. Truth that Satan, the great Deceiver, doesn't want you to know.

In their case the god of this world has blinded the minds of the unbelievers, to keep them from seeing the light of

> *the gospel of the glory of Christ, who is the image of God.* (2Cor 4:4)

He convinces you that you are in control when, in fact, you are not. Never were. He is, or was. He works you from the inside and keeps you believing that somehow you can improve yourself and be good without Christ. Fat chance. Actually no chance.

So, how does he get away with it? Well you can sum it up pretty simply as follows:

> *And no wonder, for even Satan disguises himself as an angel of light.* (2Cor 11:14)

And he does a mighty good job of it. You see, he doesn't look anything like your personal image of the Devil, whatever that is. He is just about as ordinary as apple pie. He walks by you every day in business suits and rags without being recognized. He is in the churches, synagogues, mosques, governments, schools, and right down the block. He is buried deep, joined to and enslaving the spirits of non-believers without their knowledge until Christ exposes him in His light.

The only sign you will have is that everything Satan does is for himself. If charitable giving and good works promote himself, he will be the greatest giver. If death and destruction promote himself, he isn't called the Destroyer for nothing. Whatever works.

Here is the acid test. Satan is the opposite of God. He is self for self. If it's for self-promotion, it is Satan. That might not be obvious given all the so-called good works and smiley faces out there. Do not judge by appearances.

God is Self for others. Everything he does is out of Love, even if it doesn't appear to be so. Satan may mean it for evil, but God means it for good. Again, do not judge by appearances. You must discern spiritually. How do you know? By their fruits.

> *You will recognize them by their fruits. Are grapes gathered from thornbushes, or figs from thistles?* (Matt 7:16)

XXXVIII

IN HIS IMAGE

IN GENESIS, God decided to create man, but man was to be different than anything He had created before. Man was to be made in His image. God said,

"Let us make man in our image, after our likeness ... So God created man in his own image, ..." (Gen 1:26-27)

And God said that it was very good. He even called us gods.

*I said, "You are gods,
sons of the Most High, all of you; ..."* (Ps 82:6)

Before we get the big head, note this is with a little "g." So, just how is it we are gods and made in God's image? How do we resemble our Father in heaven? We know that God doesn't have two hands and two feet so it's not a physical resemblance. God is Spirit. He has no visible form except through how He expresses Himself in His creation.

We know that God is triune. He is Father, Son, and Holy Spirit. God conceives ideas through His Spirit (Father), He expresses those thoughts through His Word (Son), and He acts on them through His Holy Spirit.

In like fashion he created man triune—spirit, soul, and body. Likewise man conceives ideas in his spirit, expresses those thoughts and speaks them (soul), and acts on them (body). Man has the ability to think, to rationalize, and make decisions. Man became conscious being aware of his surroundings. As the philosopher said, "I think, therefore I am."

In this way, we are created in the image of God, but it still doesn't portray the whole picture. There is a big difference between the big "G" and the little "g," between the "*I AM THAT I AM*" and the "I am." In order to see the difference, we need to know who God really is and who we are. From Scripture, we know that God is:

... *Love* (1John 4:8)
... *Light* (1John 1:5)
... *Wisdom* (1Cor 1:30)
... *Strength* (Hab 3:19)
... *the Way, the Truth, and the Life* (John 14:16)
... *Righteousness, Gracious, Merciful* (Ps 145)
... *Good* (1Tim 4:4)

First of all, it is important to point out that though we may think these are attributes we as people have, these are NOT attributes of God. These are who he IS. For instance, if God is Love, that means Love is God. If God is Wisdom, then Wisdom is who God *IS*.

Ready? How do we stack up? Let's start with love. Are we that kind of Love that God is, the agape love that pours itself out selflessly for others without thought of something in return, or is ours a selfish kind of love? One that heats up with passion only to meet the cooled ashes of divorce courts? I think we will lose that one. The best we can say is we have some capacity to love, but we are not in ourselves selfless love.

What about Light? Jesus said,

"I am the light of the world. Whoever follows me will not walk in darkness, but will have the light of life." (John 8:12)

Are we light? He does say of us in Matthew, "You are the light of the world. A city set on a hill cannot be hidden." That is encouraging. But we really know again that we are not light in ourselves. There is only One who is that—the I Am; the only one with life in Himself and His Son.

For as the Father has life in himself, so he has granted the Son also to have life in himself. (John 5:26)

We are lamps to hold the light. Light bearers. Without Christ, we are totally dark.

How about wisdom? I bet you know many people who think they have this one covered. However, God says in 1 Corinthians, "For the wisdom of this world is folly with God." Well ... maybe not so much.

The list goes on. We have some semblance of these things, but they are really poor imitations.

The last one up there to talk about is good. Maybe we have a chance with that one. Jesus admitted in Matthew that we were able to give good gifts, even if we were evil. That's a backhanded compliment if I ever heard one. Then He sealed it when He said in Mark 10, "Why do you call me good? No one is good except God alone." Say good-bye to the thought of being good.

You might be getting a little depressed by now, but that last little statement should really cheer you up because that is what really moves us closer to the answer. What Jesus said right there is that God is all these things. We are not. We have a built in limited version, a capacity for them, but that is not who we are. Only God is.

We were never meant to be all these things. We were meant to contain the Person who is these things. The way was provided in Christ Jesus.

And because of him you are in Christ Jesus, who became to us wisdom from God, righteousness and sanctification and redemption, ... (1Cor 1:30)

Of all the things God granted us in making us in His image, the most important is the ability to think and make choices. That is one thing that is exactly like God. With that comes risk. For instance Satan, formerly Lucifer or Light Bearer, made a choice in his delusion to believe he was all the things God is. The end result was total darkness.

For those of us who have chosen the Lord, understanding this principle takes away a huge burden. We no longer have to pretend to love, pretend to be good, pretend to be righteous. We ARE love, wisdom, and righteousness because we now contain Christ and He has replaced us. *I live, yet not I.*

I am crucified with Christ: nevertheless I live; yet not I, but Christ liveth in me: and the life which I now live in the flesh I live by the faith of the Son of God, who loved me, and gave himself for me. (Gal 2:20)

We stop trying to be what we already are. We just believe. Christ now lives on earth as us, in our individual and unique forms. There is none good but Christ. Amen.

XXXIX

IF YOU HAVE SEEN ME

IT MUST have been so marvelous to be with the Lord Jesus Christ for three years, to see all the signs and wonders that gave testimony to the Christ. Just the report of them two thousand years later continues to awe us. Yet, the disciples' view of whom their Lord really was during that tenure seems to be murky at best. Philip finally said to him,

> *"Lord, show us the Father, and it is enough for us."* (John 14:8)

Jesus then admonishes Philip in His loving way saying,

> [9] *"Have I been with you so long, and you still do not know me, Philip? Whoever has seen me has seen the Father.*

How can you say, 'Show us the Father'? ¹⁰Do you not believe that I am in the Father and the Father is in me? The words that I say to you I do not speak on my own authority, but the Father who dwells in me does his works. ¹¹Believe me that I am in the Father and the Father is in me, or else believe on account of the works themselves." (John 14:9-11)

There it was. All spelled out. Yet, this shouldn't have been a newsflash. He had been saying it all along in so many words. Maybe the disciples were just like us—a little slow and hard of hearing.

Remember when Jesus asked his disciples?

"But who do you say that I am?" (Matt 16:15)

Simon Peter replied,

"You are the Christ, the Son of the living God." (Matt 16:16)

Jesus answered him,

"Blessed are you, Simon Bar-Jonah! For flesh and blood has not revealed this to you, but my Father who is in heaven." *(Matt 16:17)*

Apparently that wasn't enough. Further revelation was required.

Remember what Jesus told them earlier?

"I and the Father are one." (John 10:30)

Maybe that didn't quicken either, but there were some who were listening. Some of the Jews knew what he was saying. They picked up stones to stone him. (John 10:31)

Jesus asked them,

> *"I have shown you many good works from the Father; for which of them are you going to stone me?"* (John 10:32)

Then the Jews answered him.

> *"It is not for a good work that we are going to stone you but for blasphemy, because you, being a man, make yourself God."* (John 10:33)

And so that is true. He was God. In the beginning was the Word, and the Word was with God, and the Word was God (John 1:1).

But he drew a distinction between Himself and the Father. He said,

> *"... for the Father is greater than I."* (John 14:28)

Admittedly, it does seem like a word game. A bit confusing. He is not the Father, but if you have seen Him, you have seen the Father. Why?

Because He was in union with the Father. The Father dwelt IN Him and He dwelt IN the Father. He was One with the Father. If you have seen one, you have seen the other. He is the radiance of the glory of God and the exact imprint of his nature, ... (Heb 1:3). He was the Word—the second Person of the trinity who was the perfect expression of the Father.

Now he peels away any further doubt. He stripped away all the outward appearances and revealed Himself.

But it's not as though His words were accepted by everyone. In His hometown, they said,

> *"Where did this man get this wisdom and these mighty works? Is not this the carpenter's son? Is not his mother called Mary? And are not his brothers James and Joseph*

and Simon and Judas? And are not all his sisters with us? Where then did this man get all these things?" And they took offense at him. (Matt 13:-57)

The Jews constantly attacked Him for making statements like these. Jesus called out their hypocrisy.

"For John came neither eating nor drinking, and they say, 'He has a demon.' The Son of Man came eating and drinking, and they say, 'Look at him! A glutton and a drunkard, a friend of tax collectors and sinners!' Yet wisdom is justified by her deeds." (Matt 11:19)

That means truth needs no champion. *"Whoever has seen me has seen the Father."* That was bold. That summed it up.

In the same way, those who are in Christ Jesus can make a similar bold statement. Let's put it like this:

Whoever has seen me has seen Christ.

"Whoa ... wait a minute," you say. "You make yourself as Christ? Don't we know your mother and father? Your sister and brothers? Aren't you a glutton and drunkard? A friend of sinners? Don't you have a demon? Where is that in the Bible?"

Well, maybe I don't fit your image of Christ that is being formed in all of us (Gal 4:19). Maybe it makes me wonder sometimes. Maybe I feel like I have a demon sometimes. If you are judging by appearances, it's impossible to see. The evidence to the contrary is daunting. But faith totally disregards appearances and feelings. It knows that scripture cannot be broken (John 10:35).

Before vocalizing *"Whoever has seen me has seen the Father,"* Jesus had already said it in so many other words regarding His relationship with the Father. The disciples just didn't get it. So also the Bible speaks the same thing regarding our relationship with Christ. Most Christians today don't get it. But there are many moments when we have to call those things that be not as though they are (Rom 4:17). It's called faith—believe. We simply reckon it to be so despite appearances or feelings to the contrary.

Just as Jesus said He was in the Father and the Father was in Him and that He and the Father were one, so also He said He was in us and we were in Him and we were one. He was unveiling the mystery which is Christ in us (Col 1:27), the mystery hidden for ages and generations but now revealed to his saints (Col 1:26)

"I do not ask for these only, but also for those who will believe in me through their word, [21] that they may all be one, just as you, Father, are in me, and I in you, that they also may be in us, so that the world may believe that you have sent me. (John 17:20-21)

Paul puts it best. He says we are ONE with Christ because ...

But he who is joined to the Lord becomes one spirit with him. (1Cor 6:17)

Our spirit is in union with His Spirit forming one spirit, not two. He in us. We in Him. We are NOT Christ but we are now individual expressions of Christ in human form, just as He was the expression of the Father in human form. The only difference is the difference between vine and branch (John 15:5). When we come to understand this, then we can say like Paul ...

I am crucified with Christ: nevertheless I live; yet not I, but Christ liveth in me: and the life which I now live in the flesh I live by the faith of the Son of God, who loved me, and gave himself for me. (Gal 2:20)

That is as bold as it gets. He lives, yet not Paul (you, me), but Christ lives in me (you). Christ lives His life in us, expressing Himself as us. Our portion is simply to believe.

www.ingramcontent.com/pod-product-compliance
Lightning Source LLC
Chambersburg PA
CBHW052032070526
44584CB00016B/2014